Making Music on the O

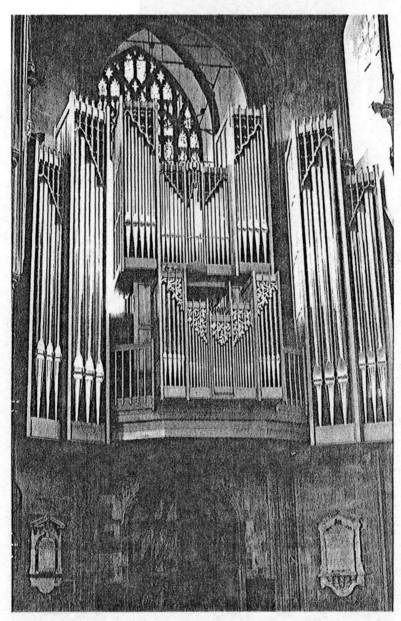

The organ in the church of St Peter Mancroft, Norwich, built on the classic *werk* principle by Peter Collins in 1984. The three manual divisions—dominated by the high, central *Hauptwerk*—are bounded on either side by the towers of the divided *Pedalwerk*. The projecting *Positiv* case hides the console behind, and just visible are some of the pipes belonging to the small *Brustwerk* above the player's head. (See text and Fig. 5 on pages 22 and 23.)

Photograph by Kenneth Ryder

Making Music
on the
Organ

Peter Hurford

revised edition

Oxford   New York
Oxford University Press

OXFORD
UNIVERSITY PRESS

Great Clarendon Street, Oxford OX2 6DP

Oxford University Press is a department of the University of Oxford.
It furthers the University's objective of excellence in research, scholarship,
and education by publishing worldwide in

Oxford New York

Athens Auckland Bangkok Bogotá Buenos Aires Calcutta
Cape Town Chennai Dar es Salaam Delhi Florence Hong Kong Istanbul
Karachi Kuala Lumpur Madrid Melbourne Mexico City Mumbai
Nairobi Paris São Paulo Shanghai Singapore Taipei Tokyo Toronto Warsaw

and associated companies in Berlin Ibadan

Oxford is a registered trade mark of Oxford University Press
in the UK and in certain other countries

Published in the United States
by Oxford University Press Inc., New York

© Peter Hurford 1988, 1990

The moral rights of the author have been asserted

Database right Oxford University Press (maker)

Reprinted 2000

ISBN 0-19-816207-3 (Pbk.)

Printed in Great Britain
on acid-free paper by
Bookcraft (Bath) Short Run Books
Midsomer Norton

PREFACE

In the course of preparing this paperback edition of *Making Music on the Organ*, I have taken the opportunity of making some textual amendments and additions, the more extended of which are contained in three new Appendices. The first of these describes the workings of a late eighteenth-century organ, and shows how the principles of good organ design have changed little in 200 years. The second describes the evolution of the swell-box, and gives guidance as to its musical use and pitfalls to be avoided. Appendix III deals with Temperament, and here I am grateful to Ann Bond for her generous assistance in helping to present a complex subject clearly, yet with such brevity.

Several readers have been kind enough to suggest that I might extend my brief to include the interpretation of other important schools of organ music, such as Italian and Spanish. But if these, then why not include Flemish and English, or the Romantic or Modern music of so many worthwhile schools as well? However, the purpose of this present book (expanded in the Introduction) is not to be an encyclopaedia of interpretation, but rather to offer some aid or encouragement to those who sense that an instrument with such a long pedigree must surely possess more musical potential than often they seem to hear. I have sought to address the reader with the objectivity of a musician for whom the organ is but one aspect of music-making; and I have tried to provide a glimpse of possibilities, to challenge standards in the player, and to encourage critical appreciation in the listener.

The only composer to have provided the organ with a large corpus of music encompassing technical perfection and great spiritual breadth is J. S. Bach. He is also the only composer to whom I myself, after a lifetime of playing and record-ing music by numerous others, constantly return with renewed anticipation of refreshment, challenge, and learning. So for me, Bach is by far the most viable linchpin for such an endeavour as this book represents, and hence is accorded the most space. I have included the French school that gave him inspiration—and the world so much sense of organ colour—because it complements and illustrates the musical essence and scope of this most difficult of instruments. Given my particular task, no other men or schools are necessary, except as passing lights to illuminate the artistic context of the organ from that day to this.

I am greatly indebted to the many people who have helped either with the original book or with this new paperback edition, by giving freely of advice, comment, and criticism, or by lending encouragement when resolution needed strengthening. In particular, I would like to thank Peter Collins, Victoria Frampton, Chris Hazell, Edward Higginbottom, Peter le Huray, Paul Keene, Hugh McLean, Richard Marlow, Christine O'Donoghue, Lydia Smallwood, and my wife Pat, with whom so many of my thoughts have been tried, argued, and honed. I was fortunate in persuading John Brennan to contribute some of his inimitable line drawings; and I am grateful to Diana Dean, who for the original edition converted seemingly endless reams of longhand into impeccable copy. Nevertheless, even with so much kind assistance, some error or shortcoming may still lurk amongst the pages which follow, and the responsibility for any such unhappiness must, of course, rest firmly with me.

Peter Hurford

St Albans,
January 1990

CONTENTS

Note on Usage   ix

Introduction   1

1. The Organist's Place in Musical Performance   5
Integrity of Musician and Instrument   6
The Organ's unique characteristics   8
Problems for the Travelling Performer   10

2. How the Organ Works   14
Working Essentials   14
The Action of Key Mechanisms   15
The Axis of Pipes   18
Architectural Layout   20
Organ-pipes   24
Sound Quality and Tonal Design   29
Changes of Colour and Dynamic: Registrational Aids   35
The Tremulant   37

3. A Basic Physical Approach to the Organ   40
Balance and Posture   40
Physical Symptoms of Nervous Tension   41
Co-ordination and an Approach to the Keyboard   42
Hints on Clothing   49

4. The Technical Basis of Movement and Expression   52
Pipe Speech   52
Touch, Time, and Silence: The Techniques of Musical Projection   53
1. Silence and Comparative Touch   55
2. Inequality and Agogic Accentuation   60
3. Rubato   67

5. Some Thoughts on Interpretation   69
Introduction   69
Some Technical Considerations in Performing Baroque Organ Music   73
(a) Musical Line   73
(b) Fingering and 'Phrasing'   74
(c) Dialogue   79

6. Towards a Grounding in Bach Interpretation 90
   Harmonic Structure 91
   Bach's Musical Line 93
   Rhythm, Pulse, and Tempo 102
   Hints on Ornamentation 107
   Hints on the Registration of Bach, his Contemporaries, and his
      Immediate Predecessors 114

7. The French Classical School 119
   Musical Style 120
   The Organ, and Registration upon it 124
   Ornamentation 128

8. Renaissance 130
   The Instrument 130
   The Player 131
   The Composer 132
   Integrity and the Student's Objectives 136

APPENDICES
   I. The Working of the Organ's Keyboard Action:
      A classic illustration of the need for excellence 139
   II. The 'Swell-Box' 142
   III. A Brief Explanation of Temperament in Keyboard Tuning 144
   IV. Specifications of Organs 147

Reading List 156

Index of Works Cited 162

General Index 164

NOTE ON USAGE

The pitch system adopted throughout is as follows:

An open pipe measuring just under eight feet from the bottom of its mouth to the top of the pipe will yield the note C, two octaves below c¹. This is the lowest key on the organ's keyboard, hence the use of the abbreviation 8′ to describe the pitch of the entire rank.

Where mention is made of a Bach work, the main title is followed by the number given in Schmieder's thematic index (see Reading List), and then by the number of the movement, where applicable: e.g. Sonata V (BWV 529) (iii).

Introduction

THIS is a book about making music; and making it on an instrument which, in its long history, has successively been revered and reviled, ravaged and reformed. It is a book written by a player, for those who are curious as to the organ's musical potential, whether players or listeners. It is not a musicological treatise, neither is it a primer; there are numerous books and articles which delve in depth into the instrument's history, or which discuss organ design or interpretational matters, while various countries each have favourite books of exercises to help students in their search for technical proficiency. Rather is it meant for the encouragement and inspiration of those who are attracted by the pipe-organ, yet find it full of problems which all too often seem to defy their attempts at music-making.

The organ's evolutionary tree bore its most abundant fruit in the century spanned by Dieterich Buxtehude (b. 1637) and J. S. Bach (d. 1750), by Guillaume Nivers and François Couperin, though by the end of Bach's life the steady dissipation of the organ's disciplined glory was well under way. However, its century of greatness established precedents of musical excellence in the design and construction of instruments, in repertory which explores and fulfils the organ's unique potential, and in performing techniques, none of which, in principle, have been compromised by the organ's somewhat chequered subsequent history. The characteristics of organ tone are the same as ever they were, and convincing musical performance in the late twentieth century still presupposes the player's ability to project intelligently articulated musical line with clarity, expressiveness, and idiomatic style; while the repertory which best exemplifies both the need for such technique and the way to achieve it is still typified by the two principal schools of the organ's greatest era.

Yet such a convenient summary must not be allowed to obscure the fact that the German and French organ styles had a common ancestry. Even the most casual delving into the organ's earlier history will reveal the seminal importance of the northern Netherlands: its influence in the sixteenth century upon the development of the classical French and Spanish organ; the export of organ-building expertise to Germany (whence came in return, a century or more later, the builders of so many of Holland's own great historic instruments); and its composers, headed by Sweelinck.

The musician of the early 1600s—and particularly the student—was already accustomed to travelling freely across the shifting political boundaries of

'Europe',[1] with the result that there was much intermingling of musical form and style. For example, Italian forms and the figuration techniques used by the English virginalists were both absorbed in the music of Sweelinck; in its turn, Sweelinck's teaching came to exert a powerful influence on composition in seventeenth-century northern Germany. And again, a century later, Bach's music would have been infinitely poorer if he had been unacquainted with such music as that of Vivaldi and Corelli, or of Couperin and Raison, let alone with the styles of his own northern neighbours, whose brilliant multi-sectioned preludes and fugues owed much to the fantasy style of Frescobaldi.

Such historical matters are part of the fabric of musical experience from which interpretative and performing techniques are developed. Although they are not of primary concern in the pages that follow, the student will find that a reasonably wide knowledge of the musical and sociological background to his art (including an awareness of parallel artistic fields) can be of practical use in determining interpretative style.

From the mid-eighteenth century, changes in musical style were accompanied by a diminishing interest in the organ. Its decline was marked by a gradual increase in size (with two stops where previously one had sufficed) and by players becoming less selective in their choice of tone colour. After the passage of a century, during which the organ was neglected by all major composers save Mendelssohn, came technical experiment, encouraged by an interest in machines brought about by the Industrial Revolution. New key actions—operated first by pneumatic, then by electric power—were invented, and with the advent of successful servo-systems came the possibility of higher wind-pressures and more decibels.[2] When eventually it was realized that servo-systems allowed the console to be placed apart from the instrument in some more socially convenient location, the demise of the organ as a viable instrument for interpretative

---

[1] A popular drinking-song of the time (the tune of which was borrowed by Sweelinck for a set of keyboard variations) referred to a 'fly', the contemporary slang for a student, flitting from one place of learning to another.

More palatino bibimus; ne gutta supersit
Unde suam possit musca levare sitim.
Sic bibimus, sic vivimus
In Academicis.

We drink in the grand manner; let not a drop | be left from which a fly could quench his thirst. | So we drink, and so we live in Academia.

[2] A mid-nineteenth-century emphasis upon increased ceremonial in the English church led to robed choirs occupying the chancel, and to organs crammed into side-chapels near the singers; increasing the pressure of pipe-wind (a measure which markedly reduces tonal subtlety) was one way of attempting to force sound out of an organ inhibited by masonry and by a *multum in parvo* optimism engendered by more money than sense.

performance was complete. The organ became more and more a liturgical convenience and an instrument whose principal attractions lay in a grand noise. It is hardly surprising, in consequence, that listeners born into such a tradition, and with no knowledge or experience of the organ as an artistic medium, should have looked upon it as mechanical (in the pejorative sense) and regarded the organist as the operator of a machine; or should have associated the organ with church functions, and seen it as an instrument suited to aural effect—principally schmaltzy or bombastic. '[Loudness] is an effect that the overwhelming majority of the public still expects from the player even today. At the end, it must roar, so that one is "simply overcome".'[3] But effects, when produced for their own sake, are self-propagating, because an effect can satisfy only in the short term, leading to the necessity for adding another, and another. . . .

Until the end of World War II, perhaps the most prized virtue of an organist was digital virtuosity. Beauty of musical line, translucent contrapuntal texture, aesthetically enhancing colours, to say nothing of articulative detail—all these were musical mysteries of little concern to the organist. In the world of popular music, however, the organ thrived. In the early years of the twentieth century the large organs built for the civic halls of thriving industrial cities brought transcriptions of orchestral works to those who rarely, if ever, had the opportunity of hearing them in their true colours. In the 1920s and 1930s the organ replaced the piano in accompaniments to silent films, and after the introduction of 'talkies' remained as an entertainment feature in its own right. As a medium for artistic interpretation, however, it was by then infinitely far removed from the organ of Bach and Couperin, or even of César Franck; the only remaining common feature was that both types of instrument had pipes which were blown by wind and played from keyboards. The theatre organ even had its own generic sounds, the whole overlaid by a constant tremolo. From my own experience when earning pin-money as a student, use of this breed of instrument was limited to a basically homophonic style of playing. Counterpoint (for which the classical organ is a perfect medium) was a foreign style to which the theatre organ was totally unsuited in the quality of its pipe-voicing, its system of 'winding', and the often rough regulation of its action. Although sufficient for the modern style, it was the wrong instrument for the classical repertory, for which it was never intended.

Since the advent of the organ renaissance in the 1930s the classical pipe-organ has gradually been restored to the mainstream of music-making. Instruments inspired by the technical precepts of the greatest builders and musicians of the

---

[3] Hermann Keller, *Die Orgelwerke Bachs* (Leipzig, 1948); trans. H. Hewitt as *The Organ Works of Bach* (Peters: London, 1967), p. 47.

organ's history, and on which the making of music is a pleasure to player and audience alike, now exist world-wide. With no disparagement of the handful of great master builders of the nineteenth century, there are today a few new instruments which challenge the player to a higher degree of *musical artistry* than has been possible since perhaps the eighteenth century.

I believe, however, that the fusion of music, instrument, and interpretative performance integral to true renaissance has yet to be achieved. This book is intended to be of some assistance towards an understanding of the artistic potential of the classical organ, its music, and its players.

It is a book of guide-lines—suggestions based upon the fruit of personal experience—and in every subject touched upon, further reading is much to be encouraged. Likewise, the reader should never forget that at the root of good performance lies constant practice and musical experiment. Student organists often evince the greatest reluctance to practise exercises which pianists regard as essential; but just as the techniques inherent in scales, arpeggios and sequential patterns of various kinds are the common currency of *all* tonal music, so should they be the common concern of *all* keyboard players. The confidence won by achieving a fluent repertoire of such exercises, rendered with consistent fingering and technical aplomb, lends an extra dimension to the pleasures of exploring touch and articulation and those other countless subtleties which contribute to expressiveness in musical line.

The organ is a musical instrument upon which men and women equally can excel; and many of the best players of my acquaintance are women. The fact that I refer throughout to players as male should therefore be understood only as a literary convenience. Likewise, in referring to 'the student' I am using the term in its broadest sense. Study is the outward expression of that healthy curiosity which keeps the artistic soul alive; it is not confined to youth, nor is the need for it ended by any examination, however prestigious.

By the same token, the amateur has as much artistic incentive to study as the professional (though perhaps at a less intense level). Indeed, in music that is within his technical competence, the amateur may sometimes communicate at a profound level; while the professional's performance can be aesthetically remote through over-concern with bravura or interpretational detail.

Thus, what I have to say is warmly addressed to the amateur—in the original and best sense of the word: the lover of the organ and its music, whether composer, player, or listener, young or old, newly curious or a lifelong captive. All that is required is an open mind, and a willingness to be challenged.

I

The Organist's Place in Musical Performance

> Keyboardists whose chief asset is mere technique are clearly at a dis-
> advantage . . . They overwhelm our hearing without satisfying it and
> stun the mind without moving it. A mere technician, however, can
> lay no claim to the rewards of those who sway in gentle undulation
> the ear rather than the eye, the heart rather than the ear, and lead it
> where they will.
>
> (C. P. E. Bach, *Essay on the True Art of Playing Keyboard Instruments*)

THE nature of music and its effect upon the spirit has inspired numerous essays, poems, analogies, and comments throughout the ages. The fact that its effect (varying from listener to listener) cannot be analysed beyond recognizable technical features has led men to describe it as 'the divine art'—a phenomenon which defies identification. Philosophers have tried to pin down the innumerable facets of its appeal, and the application of rhetorical theory has led in the past to analogies with language, and even to rules for composition and performance derived from rhetorical theory.[1]

Eduard Hanslick, writing in the nineteenth century, warned of the dangers of confusing speech with music, and of allying them too closely in terms of rhetoric: 'The fundamental difference consists in this,' he stated: 'while *sound* in *speech* is but a sign, that is, a *means* for the purpose of expressing something which is quite distinct from its medium; *sound* in *music* is the *end*, that is, the ultimate and absolute object in view'.[2]

The performer who relies for his interpretation solely upon musicological precept and digital dexterity will succeed only in communicating signs. If he has no curiosity for music's mysterious effect upon the soul, and plays without love, even his best technical efforts will succeed only in a momentary dazzling of his listeners. If, as well, he is an organist, with a formidable armoury of sound and

---

[1] See Peter Williams, 'Need Organists Pay Attention to Theorists of Rhetoric?', *The Diapason* (April 1982), pp. 3–4.

[2] *Vom Musikalisch-Schönen* (Leipzig, 1854); Eng. trans. G. Cohen *The Beautiful in Music* (Novello: London, 1891), p. 94. A century earlier, Samuel Johnson had propagated a similar notion: 'Language is only the instrument of science, and words are but the signs of ideas.' *Dictionary of the English Language* (1775).

signs at his disposal, his performance may well resemble Macbeth's 'tale Told by an idiot, full of sound and fury, Signifying nothing'. Of all instruments, the organ contains the most traps and pitfalls for the unwary performer.

Convincing musical performance calls for an amalgam of dexterity, interpretational technique, and projection (or musical persuasiveness). Projection is a skill necessary for the orator as well as for the musician, and certain basic technique is common to both: accented consonants, musically rounded vowels, tempo, and appropriate silences are the common technical stock of anyone wishing to communicate with others in a convincing manner. To the organist, whose notes have no 'dying fall', such techniques are vital, for nothing is so stultifying to music as a miasma of uninflected sounds, connected by unbroken legato.

Perhaps the most important technique that the orator and the musical performer have in common is an awareness of the listener's involvement and reaction. 'Above all things', writes Aaron Copland, 'composers and interpreters want listeners who lend themselves fully to the music that they are hearing. . . . Music can only be really alive when there are listeners who are really alive. But the listener must first develop some understanding of the music and its medium and must be able to recognize what, exactly, the interpreter is doing to the composition at the moment that he recreates it';[3] to this end the performer's knowledgeable and sensitive interpretation, together with intelligent and loving projection, must be the first ingredient in musical performance.

Integrity of Musician and Instrument

The closest musical counterpart to the orator is the singer, whose instrument—subject to the moods and humours of the body, mind, and heart—is contained within him. The singer is able literally to perform from the heart, with all the spontaneous expressiveness that this implies. Whereas other musical performers have to learn such techniques as articulation or phrasing, the singer studies them as aids to understanding rather than as devices of artifice; for phrasing is given a practical slant by the demands of breathing and by the sense of the words, while articulation is helped by the natural (and changing) sounds of vowel and consonant. Instrumental musicians, on the other hand, have to learn how to use consonants and vowels, and to them, accent and phrasing are often more a matter

[3] *What to Listen for in Music* (McGraw-Hill: New York and London, 1957), pp. 273–5. Benjamin Britten was similarly uncompromising: '[Music] demands as much effort on the listener's part as the other two corners of the triangle, this holy triangle of composer, performer and listener.' *On Receiving the First Aspen Award*, Faber and Faber: London, 1964, p. 20.

of objective understanding than of instinctive application. This is not to imply that a singer's life is technically an easy one: merely that having an inbuilt instrument gives the singer a significant advantage over a musician whose instrument must be held, or sat at!

Because the voice is the most natural form of musical expression, all instrumental musicians would do well to relate their own manner of performance to that of the voice. Difficult or ambiguous instrumental phrases often become clear when sung, just as the musical dangers inherent in the wind player's artifice of 'circular breathing' rapidly become apparent.

Musical performance is a conversation between the player and his audience, or, more accurately, between the duality of player-and-instrument and its audience. One member of this duality without the other is as nothing; but together, player and instrument become one interpretational medium. The combination closest to the natural duality of singer-and-voice is that of the woodwind player and his instrument. The player uses his lungs, as does the singer, and his musical phrases are disciplined by the necessity of breathing. The duality may also be conceived for the violinist, who holds his instrument. But in considering keyboard instruments (which must be physically approached and sat at) we become aware of a phenomenon that is less apparent when the instrument is in intimate physical contact with the player—namely that some instruments are more responsive than others, and that interpretative performance can be qualified by the instrument's technical or tonal potential. The player is more aware of using technical expertise to counter any shortcomings in his instrument.

The nature of the keyboard instrument is also important, for a duality is more easily conceived with an instrument in which the weight of the player's touch affects the dynamic, as with the piano and to a certain extent the clavichord; the ability to play loudly or softly, at will, lends a potential for expressiveness comparable with that of the voice or the bow.

Harpsichord strings, however, are plucked, with the result that piano or forte dynamics can be produced as a reflection of arm weight only within extremely narrow limits. The expressive flexibility of the instrument is therefore much more dependent upon the player's technical skill; as the use of arm weight diminishes, the sensitivity of the fingers becomes more important.

On the organ, because of several characteristics unique to the instrument, these features are intensified, and the level of finger sensitivity and articulative skill required by the organist wishing to play in a convincingly expressive manner must be of a very high order indeed. Unfortunately, some of the characteristics of the organ that are so challenging to the musician contain also a superficially attractive quality which enables even the poor player to produce effects of passing grandiloquence: such 'music' rapidly palls, and the organ tends then to be regarded—especially by the casual listener uneducated in the art of good playing—as an instrument of questionable musical value. This phenomenon was unknown in the seventeenth and eighteenth centuries and is now fortunately passing into history; but it is still sufficiently common that every organ student should be aware of the dangers.

The Organ's Unique Characteristics

(a) Physical Size

Even a small organ is physically a large instrument; while a large organ—especially to the inexperienced player—can be either an intimidating Gargantua, or a seductive enchantress whose responses inflate her lover's ego, blinding him to his technical and musical shortcomings. Of all the possible player-and-instrument dualities, that of the organ is the most dangerously misleading, psychologically challenging, and technically demanding.

(b) Lack of a 'Dying Fall'

All other musical instruments possess a common feature, namely that the length of each note has a natural limit. Instruments blown by human lungs are dependent upon those lungs being replenished at regular intervals. The notes produced on bowed instruments are limited by the length of the bow itself, and part of a modern string player's technical armoury is the ability to sustain a long note with no apparent breaks, despite a to-and-fro movement of the bow.[4] Notes on any stringed keyboard instrument have a natural 'dying fall'. This is of shorter duration on the harpsichord than it is on the piano, with the result that legato on the harpsichord is more difficult to produce; the *plucking* of a string (as opposed to the striking of it) in itself inveighs against legato, as any guitarist will testify.

Producing legato, however, is the least of the organist's worries. In fact, his problem is often how to avoid it, for notes produced by the organ have no natural limitation to their length; once a key has been depressed, that note will continue to sound at a uniform volume until the finger (or foot) is lifted. It is therefore possible to move from one note to another with no intervening inflexion or silence.

---

[4] Baroque bows, especially those used in seventeenth-century France, were much shorter than the modern variety. The use of appropriate bows in music of the period can be an aid to our understanding of interpretation in the principal Baroque schools of composition.

The technique of playing in a clean, legato manner is the first of many for an organ student to learn. But music must breathe if it is to live, and to be intelligible it must be clearly enunciated; unremitting legato denies both these qualities. So the student must quickly appreciate that, for the organist, judicious silence has a particularly golden quality; and it is worth repeating that nothing is so productive of ennui as continuous sound, devoid of breath, and lacking inflexion. Stravinsky's famous denial of the organ's musical potential—'the monster never breathes'—would have been arguably a more accurate observation if he had addressed it to the organist rather than levelling it so uncompromisingly at the instrument![5]

(c) Uniformity of Sound Projection

The vowel sound of a pipe is constant: once the key has been depressed it is not possible to qualify the sound through a technique such as a finger-controlled vibrato. However, for wind instruments in particular, vibrato can aid the projection of an expressive musical line, and—especially in Baroque music—is one of the most important of all musical ornaments. The organ's limitations in this respect have long been recognized, and an artificially induced vibrato has been a feature of the instrument for several hundred years. The Tremulant can be a bane or a blessing, depending on the artistry and musical imagination of the organ-builder, and on the musical judgement of the performer. If too intense, or with a fast beat, it imposes itself upon the listener's consciousness to the detriment of musical line; but if subtle and caressing, it can act as a gentle breeze, wafting the scent of flowers beyond the immediate confines of the garden. The Tremulant is the most neglected of the organ's artistic devices, but also one of the most important.

Another way of modifying the organ's uniform tone is for wind to be conveyed to the pipes in such a way as to induce a natural irregularity in supply as it is drawn by successive pipes. Such a system of *free wind* audibly affects only a consecutive line of notes or chords, and has no effect on stationary notes. If well designed, however, it can lend an underlying flexibility to organ tone which will aid the projection of singing musical lines.

[5] In one of his conversations with Robert Craft, discussing the composition of his *Symphony of Psalms*, Stravinsky said: 'I thought, for a moment, of the organ, but I dislike the *legato sostenuto* and the mess of octaves in the organ, as well as the fact that the monster never breathes. It is exactly the breathing of wind instruments that is one of their greatest attractions for me.' It must be said that the state of the organ in Stravinsky's lifetime—played with a servo-action, conceived on high wind-pressures, and plagued by undisciplined tonal design—was such as to discourage any composer from using it in a musically constructive way.

(*d*) Tone Quality

The particular sound made by a pipe is determined by the organ-builder, whose artistry and craftsmanship alone are responsible for the tone quality, volume, and regulation of each pipe in relation to its neighbour. On an organ in which the pipes are poorly constructed, voiced, or regulated, the performer must use the whole armoury of his artistic skill if he is to allay the instrument's tonal defects and produce a musically satisfying performance.

(*e*) Key Action

This is the link between the heart of the player and the tonal source of his musical medium. Until the mid-nineteenth century, organs used only one type of action, consisting of thin wooden rods connecting the keys to the pallets that admit wind to the pipes. After a century of experiment and change, such mechanical (or tracker) action has returned as the norm for any organ of artistic merit; but for many years to come, organists must continue to be capable of making music to high artistic standards on organs employing some means of remote control over the tonal source. In simple terms, this means that depressing the key causes electric current to activate a magnet which opens the pallet. However, once electricity replaces wooden trackers as the motive force, the player is physically separated from the tonal source and is denied that intimate communion with his instrument which is taken for granted by every other instrumental performer. This removes a vital factor from the duality of player-and-instrument; music can still be made, but at greater cost to the performer and with considerably less artistic finesse.

Problems for the Travelling Performer

The player who journeys away from his own instrument soon finds that different organs present different challenges, any one of which can affect musical performance. All organs are different. A concert pianist knows that the instrument provided for him will be to a specification accepted by the majority of concert promoters, and catered for by a handful of respected makers. The only major variants will be the style of individual makers and the acoustic properties of the hall. For an organist, the situation is infinitely more variable.

(a) Acoustic Ambience

The organ's traditional home is the church, and in common with other wind instruments it is sensitive to its acoustic environment. In an ambience created by stone, marble, tile, or brick, even a poor organ might flower. But in the 'clear' and sometimes acoustically sterile conditions of a modern concert hall, the best instrument will often fail to reveal its true musical potential.

Timing the beginnings and ends of notes in the shaping of a musical line is especially important on the organ, as its sound lacks a natural 'dying fall'; such timing is a feature of interpretation which is greatly affected by acoustic ambience. A musical line which, in a large church, would be received by the listener as a crisply articulated legato, might in a concert hall justly be criticized as unacceptably *détaché*. The player must therefore constantly be aware of the effect a particular acoustic will have upon his projection of line, and adjust his *touch* accordingly. He must always play for his listeners, wherever they may be.[6]

(b) Different Shapes and Sizes

The organ lends itself to different shapes and sizes. Regardless of the many possible variations, however, the first essential in its design is that the sound should proceed *directly* to the listener, unimpeded by poor internal design, heavy casework, or masonry. The effective projection of organ sound is in no small measure dependent upon an open location for the instrument, combined with casework which enables the organ's many tones to be cohesive without obstructing the sound. Unfortunately these minimal conditions are—especially in churches—by no means commonly met, and in such cases the performer must often modify his interpretative techniques (e.g. articulation) simply to convey intelligible musical line to the listener.

---

[6] The almost invariable resonance of European churches—which were the cradle of the organ—could be considered some artistic compensation for the organ's lack of a 'dying fall'. However, with the development of contrapuntal repertory, that same resonance challenged the player to consider problems of intelligent projection that had previously been the concern mainly of singers. Thurston Dart (*The Interpretation of Music*, 1st edn., Hutchinson: London, 1954), p. 58 quotes J. van der Elst writing common sense about the performing of polyphony in a resonant building: '. . . when several notes are set to a single syllable, each must be articulated distinctly and with attention to detail, lest to anyone hearing them at a distance they seem blurred and little more than a continuous up-and-down humming. Melodies sung in a clear style, with this well-defined separation of the notes, reach the ear of the listener some way away in a smooth distinct flow.' (*Notae Augustianae*, 1657).

(c) Tonal Design

The tonal design of an organ (that is, the sound quality of its composite pipes) is, to the listener, its most obvious feature; but even though the tonal basis of organs has changed little in five hundred years, the possible variations from one instrument to another are so multifarious that no two organs are alike. It is principally this feature of the instrument which makes it necessary for the player, prior to his performance, to spend several hours on a strange organ; as well as getting to know the action and the effect of the building's acoustics, he must discover the organ's tonal potential and prepare appropriate registrations of those sounds which will best enable him to express the aesthetic of the music.[7]

(d) The Console

Finally, there is the apparently simple matter of the console at which the player sits and makes his music. The console is at the hub of the playing process, and the layout of its various features is central to the organist's relationship with the instrument.

Nevertheless, as with organs themselves, no two consoles are ever the same. Such basic dimensions as the shape of the keys, and the disposition of the keyboards relative to each other and to the pedalboard vary, from country to country and from one historical period to another—often, indeed, at the whim of the individual builder. Nor can the organist rely on the bench being adjustable to his own particular proportions (one dreams of the concert pianist who arrived to find a kitchen chair at his Steinway).

Then there is the sheer size of the console, which can vary from a single keyboard and a few drawstops to such an array of keyboards, stops, buttons, switches and flashing lights that the good player might well suffer nightmares, and the bad player delusions of grandeur: a palace for the ego to dwell in—a jumbo cockpit for the private flyer.

Servo-mechanisms brought in their train an enormous variety of aids to performance—first useful, then non-essential, and finally disturbing. I myself have played countless organs which have required almost as much time coping with the aids (which can differ widely in their design) as in registering the tone

[7] This is also an appropriate occasion for him to remember that the listener's critical perception is affected by the tonal quality of the instrumental medium, and by loudness. Young people have a greater tolerance of noise and of high frequency sound than their elders, for whom an aesthetically enhancing tone colour is likely to be more musically winning than the numbing experience of being 'simply overcome' by high sound levels.

colours for my concert. In such conditions the galling fact remains that, in the end, the listener wishes only to hear a musical performance and neither knows nor cares (and rightly so) about the maze of ancillary devices that may have absorbed a great deal of valuable preparation time.

Most sizeable organs of good quality being built today have mechanical key action; the number of aids to performance is kept to a useful minimum; and design effort is being devoted to such matters as the quality of action and tonal architecture within the concept of a particular musical style. In short, the best builders are designing organs with musical excellence as their priority.

Today the organist's place in musical performance is more assured than at any time since 1750, thanks to the revelations of the modern organ renaissance and an ever-increasing number of discerning listeners. The challenge now is to the organist himself; for the state of the art requires musical minds that are curious about interpretational and performing techniques, and that are filled with a regard for the listener's musical involvement.

2

How the Organ Works

For there is a music wherever there is a harmony, order or proportion.

(Sir Thomas Browne, 1605–82)

ANY performing musician should have a working knowledge of his instrument, so that at least he may be aware of the extent of its potential for music-making, as well as possessing, perhaps, sufficient technical knowledge to be able to cure minor ills prior to, or during, performance. The skill of an instrument maker he does not need; but an awareness of basic theory will give him a more sympathetic relationship with his instrument, and will contribute to that integrity of player-and-instrument that is so desirable in musical performance. This chapter provides an outline of such basic features of organ design and construction as may have some useful bearing on performance practice.

Working Essentials

The working essentials of a pipe-organ are:

a source of air under pressure (known as 'wind');[1]
a 'chest' to contain the wind, on which sits
a 'rank' of pipes (one pipe for each note of the keyboard), into which the wind is admitted by 'pallets', opened and closed by manual (or pedal) keys;
'stops' (or 'registers') to enable ranks offering various sounds to be chosen by the player.

Until the middle of the fifteenth century, large organs were commonly one immense 'mixture' of ranks, that is to say, the operation of one key caused from twenty to a hundred pipes (tuned in octaves and fifths) to sound simultaneously. This type of instrument, of which the most famous English example was the

---

[1] The difference between atmospheric pressure and the extra pressure created by mechanical means (blower and bellows) is measured by a gauge consisting of water in an open-ended U-tube; air-pressure is applied to one end of the tube, and the distance between the levels of water so displaced is a measurement of 'wind-pressure'.

tenth-century organ of Winchester Cathedral, was known as *Blockwerk*.[2] During the second half of the fifteenth century, average-sized and large organs were increasingly provided with a means of stopping the wind from entering specific ranks of pipes, giving the player a choice of sounds; hence the English term 'stops', indicating the various ranks of pipes on an organ. From 1500, players were demanding new colours—including flutes and reeds, drums and bird-song—and by the middle of the sixteenth century, larger instruments contained all the composite features of organs which would develop into the workshops and show-places of the great seventeenth- and eighteenth-century classical organ schools.

The Action of Key Mechanisms

(a) Manuals

However brilliant the tonal design of an organ, its potential for music-making rests finally on the quality of its *action*, from key to pallet. In order to achieve that ideal oneness of player and instrument, the player must be free to communicate the most sensitive nuances of touch with no physical barrier to mar the instrument's response. The only completely satisfactory form of action is one in which the movement of the player's fingers is accurately reflected in minuscule detail at the pallet; and the only means by which this may be achieved is through a purely mechanical linking of finger and tonal source—as with any other musical instrument.

From the player's point of view, factors which affect his relationship with the pallet may be summarized as follows.

1. *The surface of the keys*. Key-coverings should be of ivory, bone, or wood, and never synthetic. Plastic keys are non-absorbent, and perspiration from the fingers

---

[2] At Chartres in 1481, two *extra* keys were added, each furnished with no fewer than 105 pipes. Such instruments bring to mind W. H. Auden's *Anthem for St Cecilia's Day* (1942), in which he relates that:

> ... by ocean's margin this innocent virgin
> Constructed an organ to enlarge her prayer,
> And notes tremendous from her great engine
> Thundered out on the Roman air.

The monk Wulfstan at Winchester (where 18 keys played only 10 pipes) reported that 'like thunder the iron tones batter the ear'. *Blockwerk* must indeed have seemed very noisy when compared with all other contemporary musical instruments, and fit for St Cecilia only in her most passionate moments. One also should remember that it was probably used mainly for underlining a cantus firmus in single notes. See James W. McKinnon, 'The 10th-century Organ at Winchester', *Organ Year Book* 5 (1974), p. 4.

causes an unpleasant stickiness which inhibits the player's more subtle approach to touch.

2. *The length of the keys.* Baroque organs had shorter and slightly narrower keys, which are more convenient than modern ones for rapid passagework, especially if old fingering patterns are used. However, short keys need a more precise approach to hand-position and touch, and are therefore less forgiving than longer ones.

3. *Depth of touch.* The amount of vertical movement in the keys—a design factor set by the organ-builder—can affect the player's touch and fluency: too little movement, and the action can seem insubstantial; too much, and it becomes cumbersome. Either extreme reduces sensitivity and forces the player to use more artifice in the articulation of musical line, leading possibly to less convincing performance. Many organists consider that an ideal depth of touch was that developed by Gottfried Silbermann (1683–1753).

4. *The movement of the action.* The pressing of a key involves two interlinked processes: the resistance of the pallet, and such physical pressure as is necessary to actuate the mechanism. The pallets are situated, one to each note, inside the wind-chest and immediately underneath the rows of pipes which they serve. Thus the pallet for bottom C will admit wind to every pipe on its channel depending on whether the individual sliders (worked by the 'stops') are on or off (Fig. 1). Each pallet is opened against the pressure of wind which is constantly trying to keep it closed. As the pressure of the player's fingers on the key increases, the point is reached where it overcomes the resistance of the chest wind, and the player feels a plucking sensation. The degree of pluck will vary according to the design of the pallet and the pressure of the chest wind;[3] ideally, it should be such as to be clearly recognizable by the finger, while not so great that overcoming it results in a sudden, uncontrollable drop on to the key-bed.

In matters of articulation, the prompt cessation of a note in relation to the speech of the next one is of vital interpretative significance. The *closing* of the pallet (in which the pressure of chest wind is assisted by a spring) needs therefore to be very rapid if the player is to be successful in projecting, say, eight even staccato notes per second (semiquavers when crotchet equals 120). See *Touch* on pp. 57–8.

The weight and friction of the action's various parts should be minimal, as their effect is to disguise the feel of the pallet at the finger; so the inherent weight of the integral parts of the action at the finger should ideally be as close to zero as is practicable. Large instruments in which long runs of trackers are necessary will obviously present more problems than small ones.

---

[3] High-pressure wind (4″–12″ or more) in the chest is the reason why pure tracker organs of the Romantic era possessed such heavy key-touch; pneumatically assisted mechanisms (e.g. the Barker lever) were invented partly to overcome this problem.

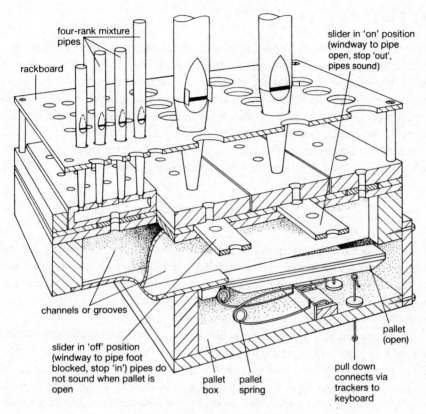

four-rank mixture pipes

rackboard

slider in 'on' position
(windway to pipe
open, stop 'out',
pipes sound)

channels or grooves

slider in 'off' position
(windway to pipe foot
blocked, stop 'in') pipes do
not sound when pallet is
open

pallet
box

pallet
spring

pallet
(open)

pull down
connects via
trackers to
keyboard

Fig. 1.   Windchest cross section

Key actions have changed only in small details since the early sixteenth century. The two most common designs are illustrated in Figs. 3 and 4. Of these, suspended action (*mécanique suspendue*), though requiring great precision in design and construction, offers the player the most sensitive response; as may be gathered from Fig. 3, and from the Dom Bédos drawing reproduced in Appendix I, it can only be employed where sufficient height is available.

One further point to be noted is the necessity for a *rollerboard* (see Fig. 2). The width of a chest containing pipes over an organ's compass is much greater than the width of the keyboard. Action from the keys must therefore be transmitted to points directly beneath their respective pallets; this is achieved through the use of rollers with an arm fixed at each end.

(b) Pedals

The action between the pedal keys and their chests consists similarly of a completely mechanical connection, the construction of which differs from manual key action in several details (none of which need concern us here). It is important to remember, however, that the precision and sensitivity of the pedal action must be comparable with that of the manuals; for the varieties of touch to be exploited by the fingers are not less carefully applied by the feet. The only concession to sensitivity is a certain spring resistance built into the pedal keys (the feet being more weighty than the fingers) lest they be too sensitive for comfort.

The Axis of Pipes

As may be seen in Fig. 2, the pipes of each rank are so arranged that their combined weight is evenly distributed on the windchest, the lowest (and heaviest) pipes being normally at either end, though sometimes in the middle as well. Thus, pipes are usually arranged in whole-tone progressions, beginning from one end of the chest with C–D–E–F♯, and from the other with C♯–D♯–F–G, etc.

These general principles of action and chest construction imply that the axis of a rank of pipes will naturally lie at right angles to the listener standing in front of the instrument (Figs. 2 and 5). This feature of the organ's construction is also musically advantageous, as the composite pipes of each rank will all be approximately the same distance from the audience, and their sound will be projected to the listener in a direct and relatively even manner. Conversely, in organs where the pipe axis lies in the same plane as the listener's perceptions (i.e. he is facing the end of the windchest instead of its front), pipes within each rank tend to obstruct each other's sound, projection can be disturbingly uneven, and musical line and articulation are less distinct.

With regard to the axis of pedal-pipechests, the considerations outlined above are much less critical than for manual pipechests, mainly because the pedals are normally used only for one line of counterpoint instead of the two, three, or four lines customarily played by the hands. However, although the musical requirements are much less complex, the sound should still be projected as directly and clearly as possible to the listener. The organ's designer must never forget that the line of counterpoint played by the feet must be in *equal partnership* with lines played by the fingers, both in directness of speech, and in volume (see p. 47).

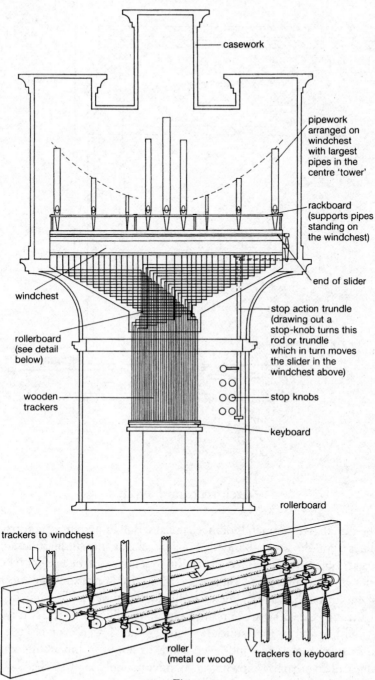

casework

pipework arranged on windchest with largest pipes in the centre 'tower'

rackboard (supports pipes standing on the windchest)

end of slider

windchest

stop action trundle (drawing out a stop-knob turns this rod or trundle which in turn moves the slider in the windchest above)

rollerboard (see detail below)

wooden trackers

stop knobs

keyboard

rollerboard

trackers to windchest

roller (metal or wood)

trackers to keyboard

Fig. 2

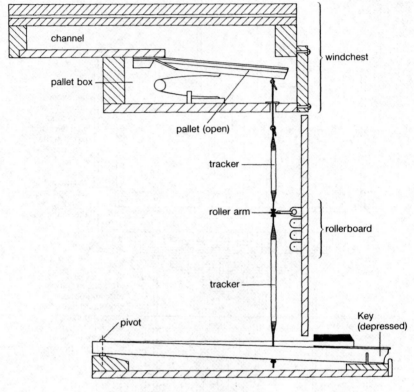

channel

windchest

pallet box

pallet (open)

tracker

roller arm

rollerboard

tracker

Key (depressed)

pivot

Fig. 3.   *Suspended action*

Architectural Layout

It can be seen that the demands of mechanical action impose strict constructional disciplines upon the organ-builder. As a general rule, the simplest design offers the greatest potential for refined and sensitive action, and the builder who strays from this precept must tread cautiously. Ingenuity in transmitting mechanical movement through corners not at right angles, though allowing perhaps a visually striking case design, can result in an action which is less responsive to the player's wishes and is mechanically troublesome. The use of electric action instead of mechanical rods and levers tends to diminish the architectural and tonal unity of an organ by allowing the builder not only to place chests where he pleases in relation to the keyboards, but also to dispense with slider-chests

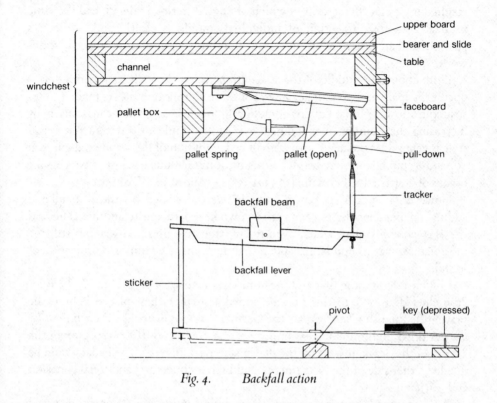

Fig. 4.   *Backfall action*

entirely, and to dispose of pipes in an *ad hoc* manner. Such opportunities—for whatever reason—are taken only at the expense of the organ's instrumental integrity, and can never be justified on musical grounds; for each indulgence runs the risk of lessening the effectiveness of projection between instrument and listener. The foremost consideration of anyone charged with building a new organ must be the proper positioning of the instrument relative to its listeners, having regard to the axis of its pipe-ranks and the constructional discipline that this entails.

The history of the organ since its diversification from *Blockwerk* has been that of an instrument which could retain its overall unity even when divided into contrasting sections, played from different keyboards. Inherent in its growth may be seen an increasing potential for dialogue, as between members of the same family; yet also for wholeness—the family standing together as an integral unit, strengthened by the compatibility of its several parts. Such disciplined unity resulted in design characteristics which, though differing in detail, had the same musical aim—the projection of individual sounds as clearly and directly as possible, and an ensemble which was given homogeneity and substance by case-work.

From about the middle of the sixteenth century, these characteristics developed principally in two parallel ways. Southern European builders tended to restrict the number of manual divisions, developing instead greater tonal variety by increasing the number of individually controlled ranks of different pitch; this style is generally associated with a small pedal division of flue- and reed-pipes at 16′ and 8′ pitch, and may be seen at its most miraculous level of artistry in the organs of Gottfried Silbermann (1653–1753; see Appendix IV, p. 150).

However, in northern Europe, organs were designed on the principle of adding independent chests, each with its own keyboard, one to another. This was the *Werkprinzip* organ, which even today, after five hundred years, is still the most natural way to build a sizeable instrument, ensuring uniform projection of sound.

In such a design, the first and most important chest of pipes is the *Hauptwerk* ('the chief division'); to this may be added a smaller chest placed behind the player (the English *Chaire* organ, the German *Rückpositiv*, or the French *Positif à dos*). A third division could be built over the *Hauptwerk* (*Oberwerk*), or in the 'breast' of the organ, just above the player's head (*Brüstwerk*). The Pedal would be divided either side of the instrument, lending it architectural and tonal cohesion and *gravitas*.

In the mature *Werkprinzip* organ, the various divisions are theoretically based on ranks of Principals (open metal pipes) of different pitch: thus, *Hauptwerk* 8′ (fundamental pitch), *Positiv* 4′ (an octave higher), *Brüstwerk* or *Oberwerk* 2′, and Pedal 16′. The decreasing pipe-lengths are reflected in tone-cabinets of diminishing size, which in turn produce a less resonant and more 'brittle' sound as they become smaller. When played together, the divisions complement each other, producing a scintillating ensemble of harmonically developed grandeur (see frontispiece and Fig. 5).

The placing of the *Positiv* division in front of, and separated from, the main organ case is vitally important for two reasons. Architecturally, its position lends visual perspective and a certain lightness to an instrument which might otherwise appear too massive. Musically, the presence of a division (second only to the *Hauptwerk* in importance) so much closer to the listener lends aural perspective which enhances the concept of *dialogue*; the consequent musical possibilities have been much explored. In the great preludes and fugues of Buxtehude and his contemporaries, the shifting aesthetic of successive sections can often benefit from a prepared registrational scheme incorporating changes of manual rather

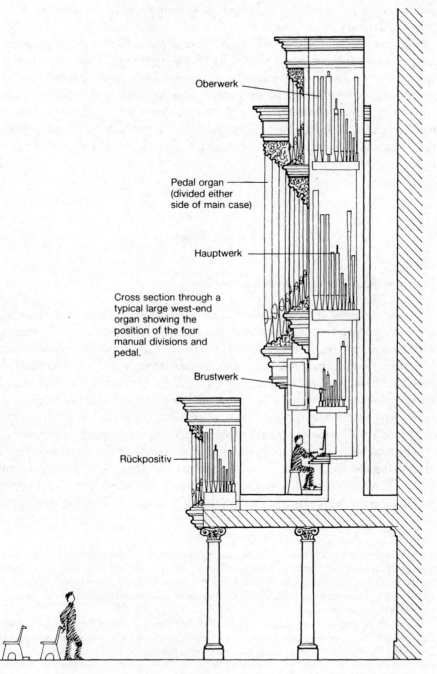

Oberwerk

Pedal organ
(divided either
side of main case)

Hauptwerk

Cross section through a
typical large west-end
organ showing the
position of the four
manual divisions and
pedal.

Brustwerk

Rückpositiv

Fig. 5

than changes of stops; the technique is known as 'terraced registration', or 'terraced dynamic'.[4]

The great Parisian organs of Louis XIV's time did not subscribe to the precise architectural divisions characterized by the *Werkprinzip* in northern Europe, apart from the *Positif à dos*, which was common in large seventeenth-century instruments. The other divisions were housed together in the main case: the Grand Orgue chest was high enough to speak over the *Postif à dos*, with the limited pedal ranks either behind or divided on either side, the short-compass Récit usually on a small chest above and in front of it, and the Echo buried beneath it.

Organ-Pipes

(a) *Open Flue-pipes (e.g. Principals or Flutes)*

When air is forced through a slit, whorls or eddies are formed in the resulting airstream, and a feeble note is created, the pitch of which depends on the speed of the airstream and the width of the slit (Fig. 6). If a narrow, pointed wedge is then inserted into the airstream, the note becomes stronger and more defined; by moving the wedge closer to or further from the slit, the pitch of this edge-tone is raised or lowered, though the optimum pitch is where the note is strongest.

The edge-tone in an organ-pipe is given musical substance by the body (or 'resonator') of the pipe, the length of which determines the pitch of its note.[5]

The basic reason for a pipe going out of tune is that when its temperature is altered, the resistance of the enclosed column of air changes. A warmer column offers less resistance to the constant pressure from the windchest, so the air will therefore move more quickly, causing the pitch to rise. The tuning is corrected

---

[4] An excellent example may be seen in the opening two sections of Buxtehude's Prelude and Fugue in F sharp minor (BuxWV 146). The passagework which opens the prelude is particularly appropriate for the *Positiv*, on which it can be expressed with clarity and brilliance; the massive chords of the following section, on the other hand, benefit from the more resonant environment of the *Hauptwerk* situated in the main case.

[5] Inside the resonator, a stationary wave-form of vibrating air is produced; the air in the middle of the pipe is still (node), while at the top and at the mouth of the pipe it has maximum freedom to move (antinodes) (Fig. 7(*b*)). In a pipe the top of which is stopped by a cap, the air is free to move only at the pipe's mouth: the node is therefore at the end of the pipe, the wave-form is halved and the pitch drops by an octave (Fig. 9).

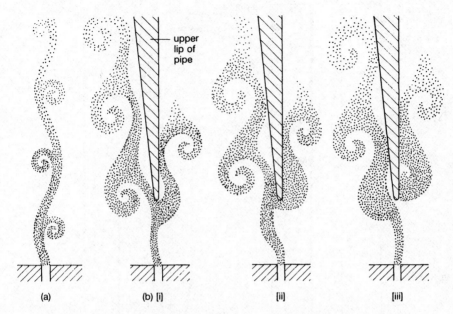

upper
lip of
pipe

(a)   (b) [i]   [ii]   [iii]

Fig. 6.   *Slit tone and edge tone showing whorls and eddies around upper lip of pipe*

by altering the length of the pipe, the most common method being the tapping up (to flatten) or down (to sharpen) of a metal slide encircling the top of the pipe (Fig. 7(*a*)). However, tuning slides are often made of different metal from the pipes themselves; in this case, temperature changes can cause the two metals to expand or contract at different rates, thereby increasing the likelihood of the slide slipping. Another cause of slipping is vibration of the instrument.

An alternative method of tuning is the coning, inwards or outwards, of the top edge of the pipe itself; this must be done only with a special tool, and never by bending the metal by hand. The advantage of cone-tuning, given the relatively stable temperature that always suits the organ best, is that the instrument shows greater tuning integrity, and the open pipes rarely need to be touched (Fig. 7(*c*)).

While the *length* of a flue-pipe's body is related to its *pitch*, its *width* (in relation to length) qualifies its *tone*. The narrower the pipe, the thinner and more 'stringy' the tone will be; conversely, wider pipes are more fluty. Amongst other

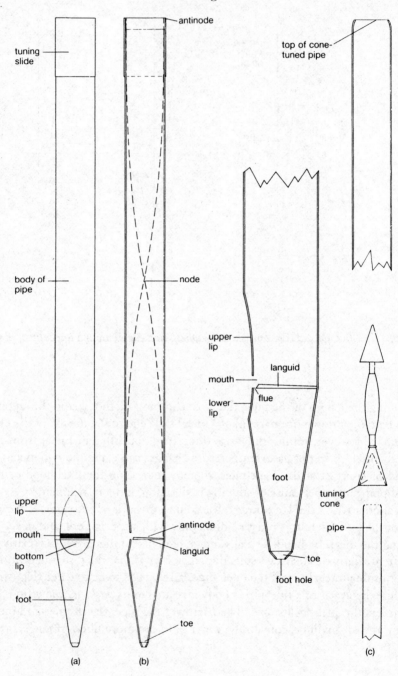

Fig. 7

factors which can affect the tone of flue-pipes are:

the metal used in their construction (heavy lead alloys produce a duller sound; zinc or tin makes the sound brighter and more 'edgy');[6]
the shape of the resonating body (see Fig. 8).

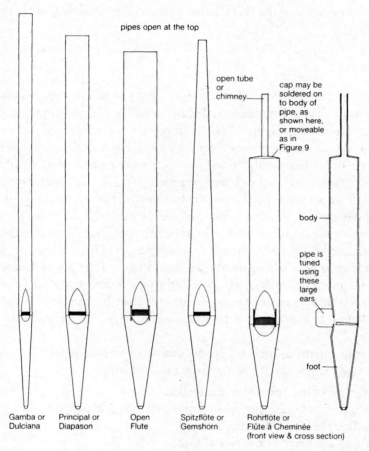

pipes open at the top

open tube or chimney

cap may be soldered on to body of pipe, as shown here, or moveable as in Figure 9

body

pipe is tuned using these large ears

foot

| Gamba or Dulciana | Principal or Diapason | Open Flute | Spitzflöte or Gemshorn | Rohrflöte or Flûte à Cheminée (front view & cross section) |

Fig. 8

(b) Stopped Flue-pipes

These are closed at their upper end, either by a cap slid over the outside of metal pipes, or by a stopper of wood and leather inserted into the top of wooden pipes.

[6] The metal most commonly used in pipe-making is an alloy of tin and lead. This pipe-metal yields the best overall reinforcement of the first seven harmonic partials. The higher the percentage of tin employed, the brighter will be the tone.

The cap or stopper has the effect of lowering the pitch of the pipe by an octave; a pipe of 4′ length will sound at 8′ pitch (Fig. 9). Tuning is effected by adjusting the position of the cap (in, sharper; out, flatter).

Some pipes are half-stopped: for example, the cap of a Chimney Flute (Rohrflöte) is pierced by an open metal tube; the pipe is then technically open, while retaining some of the characteristics (attractively modified) of the stopped pipe (Fig. 8).

(c) Reed-pipes

An airstream causes a tongue of brass (the 'reed') to vibrate either *against* the opening in a hollow brass tube (the 'shallot') or *within* it; these two types of tone source are described respectively as a 'beating reed' and a 'free reed'.

A wire tuning-spring presses the reed (which has a slight outwards curve) against the shallot; moving the spring downwards or upwards alters the vibrating length of the reed and raises or lowers the pitch (Fig. 10). The fundamental pitch of reed-pipes does not depend upon the full length of resonators in the manner of flue-pipes. As the vibrating source (the reed) itself yields definitive pitch, it is sufficient that the resonator is of a length relative to a harmonic partial of that particular note.[7] Thus, a 16′ reed may have a resonator of half, quarter, or even an eighth or sixteenth of the nominal maximum length of the pipe. However, the shorter the resonator, the less developed is the pipe's tonal output, and the more apparent becomes the rattle or buzz produced by the vibrating reed; though with careful design, such apparent drawbacks can be turned to curiously attractive advantage.

The wide variety of tone colour obtainable from reed-pipes stems from a sophisticated permutation of six constructional features:

1. the shape of the opening in the shallot;
2. the amount of curvature applied to the vibrating brass strip;
3. whether the reed is 'beating' or 'free';
4. the size and shape of the pipe's 'boot';
5. the shape and length of the pipe's resonator;
6. the material used in the construction of the pipe (i.e. the composition of the metal, type of wood, etc.).

Some examples of different resonators may be seen in Figs. 10 and 11.

---

[7] In the case of the Regal, the influence of its short resonator is diminished to such an extent that its effect upon pitch is minimal.

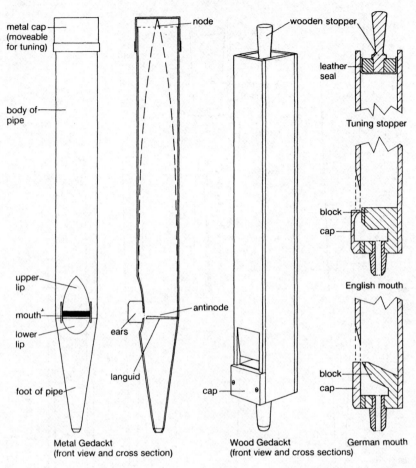

metal cap
(moveable
for tuning)

body of
pipe

node

wooden stopper

leather
seal

Tuning stopper

upper
lip

mouth

lower
lip

ears

antinode

block

cap

English mouth

languid

foot of pipe

cap

block

cap

German mouth

Metal Gedackt
(front view and cross section)

Wood Gedackt
(front view and cross sections)

Fig. 9

Sound Quality and Tonal Design

The fundamental (or audibly apparent note) of a sound contains non-audible overtones (or partials) in a mathematical progression. Sound quality may be expressed in terms of the relative strength of partials present in a particular sound. Thus the pure sound of a flute is what it is because the partials are evenly distributed in their relative strength, decreasing as they progress, though with a stronger bias towards the even-numbered partials (2, 4, 6, 8, etc.). The presence of strong odd-numbered partials (3, 5, 7, 9, etc.) makes a sound that is more reed-like,

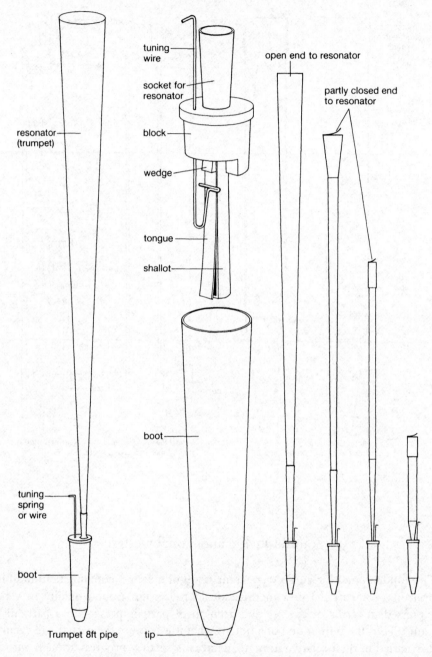

tuning wire

socket for resonator

open end to resonator

partly closed end to resonator

resonator (trumpet)

block

wedge

tongue

shallot

boot

tuning spring or wire

boot

Trumpet 8ft pipe

tip

Fig. 10.   *Four reed pipes each speaking the same note; left to right: Trumpet, Oboe, Krummhorn and Vox Humana*

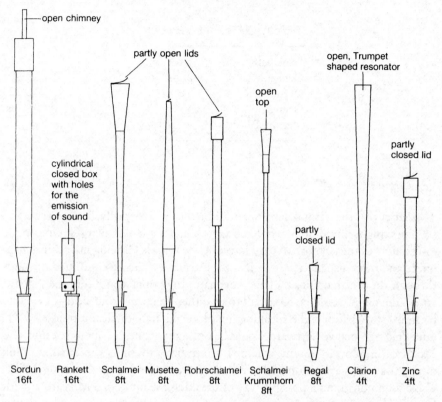

open chimney

partly open lids

open, Trumpet
shaped resonator

open
top

partly
closed lid

cylindrical
closed box
with holes
for the
emission
of sound

partly
closed lid

| Sordun 16ft | Rankett 16ft | Schalmei 8ft | Musette 8ft | Rohrschalmei 8ft | Schalmei Krummhorn 8ft | Regal 8ft | Clarion 4ft | Zinc 4ft |

Fig. 11.   *Various reed stops, all pipes drawn to the same scale*

or hollow (like that of the clarinet). A prevalence of strong upper partials causes the sound to be more 'edgy' and cutting.[8]

(a) Principals, or Diapasons

Open pipes that are neither wide nor narrow possess an even distribution of lower and higher partials and form the principal basis of organ tone, hence their generic name—Principals, or Diapasons. A chorus of Principals, based upon an 8′ fundamental rank, may be made up as in Table 1.

---

[8] The highest partial that can be obtained from a pipe is the one that has a wavelength four times the diameter of the pipe; it is for this reason that narrow pipes possess higher partials than wide ones and will have a thinner and more 'stringy' tone.

Table 1. Chorus of Principals

Principal	$8'$
Octave	$4'$
Quint	$2\frac{2}{3}'$
Octave	$2'$
Mixture IV–V	$[1']$

(b) Mixtures

The Mixture is the natural descendant of *Blockwerk*. Normally, between two and six pipes might sound on one note, the speaking length of the largest pipe on the lowest note of the keyboard (two octaves below middle C) being no lower than $2'$ pitch, and more usually $1\frac{1}{3}'$ or $1'$. If these pitches were to be continued upwards through the entire compass of the keyboard, the point would soon be reached where the pipes would be too small to be either practical or musical—or even to be heard (for example, the speaking length of the hypothetical top note of a $1'$ rank on a five-octave keyboard would be only .375 inches, or about 9.5 mm!). So Mixtures employ a system whereby from time to time the smallest rank disappears and a larger one takes its place; this is known as 'breaking back'.[9] Table 2 demonstrates a possible way of breaking the ranks of a Mixture $1'$ with four ranks in the bass increasing to five in the extreme treble where more power and definition is required. Note that the $1'$ rank continues unbroken from the lowest C to d^3 (the highest note on many Baroque organs); and that the $2'$ rank is continuous in the treble part of the mixture, from middle C upwards; this gives continuity through the 'breaks'.

Table 2. Breaking the ranks of a Mixture

	$4'$	$2\frac{2}{3}'$	$2'$	$1\frac{1}{3}'$	$1'$	$\frac{2}{3}'$	$\frac{1}{2}'$	$\frac{1}{3}'$
At bottom C					$1'$,	$\frac{2}{3}'$,	$\frac{1}{2}'$	$\frac{1}{3}'$
c				$1\frac{1}{3}'$,	$1'$,	$\frac{2}{3}'$,	$\frac{1}{2}'$	
(middle) c$'$			$2'$,	$1\frac{1}{3}'$,	$1'$,	$\frac{2}{3}'$		
g^1		$2\frac{2}{3}'$,	$2'$,	$1\frac{1}{3}'$,	$1'$			
d^2	$4'$,	$2\frac{2}{3}'$,	$2'$,	$1\frac{1}{3}'$,	$1'$			
d$\sharp^3$	$4'$,	$2\frac{2}{3}'$,	$2'$,*	$1\frac{1}{3}'$				

* This rank is doubled by another of the same pitch.

[9] 'Break-back' is also applied, of course, to any individual rank of $1'$ pitch or higher.

(c) Flutes

In the design of an organ, consideration of the Principal chorus has first priority. Some Flutes may then be incorporated, of which the 8′ rank would probably be stopped, or partially stopped, while the 4′ might well be open. The addition of a 16′ stopped rank would add gravity to the Principal chorus; for this reason it was an important component of the *plein jeu* of the French classical period (see Chapter 7).

At this point it should be noted that Flute ranks of a pitch higher than 4′ as a general rule tend not to mix well with Principals. A diagrammatic outline of various pipes in increasing order of width and flutiness may be seen in Fig. 8 (note that they all sound the same pitch).

(d) Mutations

Just as certain combinations of harmonic partials yield different tonal qualities, so ranks of organ-pipes whose fundamental pitches follow the sequence of the harmonic series may be combined to create characteristic synthetic timbres of their own. Open Flutes coalesce in a far more effective and colourful manner than Principals to create homogeneous new tone colours, and the characteristic French organ of the late seventeenth century, more than any other style of instrument, demonstrates this technique in a uniquely mature manner. For example, the Cornet is a unified and homogeneous combination of various Flutes at 8′, 4′, $2\frac{2}{3}′$, 2′, and $1\frac{3}{5}′$ pitches (the first five harmonic partials—see Table 3). If from this combination the 4′ and the 2′ were to be deleted, we would still be left with the odd-numbered partials 1, 3, and 5, the tonal characteristic of which is a hollow, reedy sound: indeed it is the third and fifth partials that are mainly responsible for the rich, piquant, and almost reedy character of the Cornet. For sparkling sounds, the even-numbered partials are of most help, yielding 8′ plus any permutation of 4′, 2′, $1\frac{1}{3}′$, 1′ at the player's whim (note that the omission of 4′ and 2′ would leave a predominance of upper partials, thus producing a sharper and more piquant sound).

The north European organs of the seventeenth and eighteenth centuries made far less use of the homogeneous qualities of wide-scale Flute mutations than did their southern neighbours or their French counterparts. Their preference for the more cutting edge of narrow-scaled pipes at $2\frac{2}{3}′$ and $1\frac{1}{3}′$ pitch took the form of a combination of both ranks in a stop known as the Sesquialtera; this, when combined with an 8′ stopped Flute (Gedackt) and sometimes a 4′ Flute as well, became one of the most popular registrations for solo lines in chorale preludes and similar works.

Table 3. Harmonic Partials and Organ Pitch

Partial	Name of audible note* (assuming the fundamental to be C)	Organ pitch
1	C	$8'$
2	c	$4'$
3	g	$2\frac{2}{3}'$
4	c^1	$2'$
5	e^1	$1\frac{3}{5}'$
6	g^1	$1\frac{1}{3}'$
7	a♯	$1\frac{1}{7}'$
8	c^2	$1'$
9	d^2	$\frac{8}{9}'$
10	e^2	$\frac{4}{5}'$
12	g^2	$\frac{2}{3}'$
15	b^2	$\frac{8}{15}'$
16	c^3	$\frac{1}{2}'$
24	g^3	$\frac{1}{3}'$
32	c^4	$\frac{1}{4}'$
48	g^4	$\frac{1}{6}'$
64	c^5	$\frac{1}{8}'$
96	g^5	$\frac{1}{12}'$
128	c^6	$\frac{1}{16}'$

* Except for the octaves, note-names are approximate.

Note   It is unusual for ranks of pipes smaller than $1'$ pitch to be individually controllable, though the smaller 5ths and octaves frequently occur in Mixture stops. It was the custom in the classical Italian organ for 5ths and octaves to be separately ranked down to $\frac{1}{4}'$. The limit of pitch in the Mixture-work of the seventeenth-century French organ was $\frac{1}{8}'$, or a speaking length of about $1\frac{1}{2}$ inches. The shortest practical speaking length of an organ pipe is $\frac{1}{16}'$ or $\frac{1}{4}''$.

Changes of Colour and Dynamic: Registrational Aids

One of the first requirements in convincing music-making is an attractive instrumental sound which woos the ear; ideally, its quality will also be perfectly matched to the mood (or aesthetic) of the music, from which indeed it is sometimes inseparable.

The organist, however, must accept the sounds offered by the organ on which he is to play, and use them in the service of the music with all the art of which he is capable. This process is occasionally rewarding, but is more frequently fraught with frustration. However, a few principles may be determined as guidelines.

The establishing of a yardstick in sound quality is a vital part of the organist's education; and the garnering of experience, particularly of instruments associated with specific periods of composition, is much to be recommended. The quality of sound in fine, historic organs, or in the best modern ones, is often so appropriate to the music and so attractive to the ear that changes of registration in the course of single movements (especially if written before 1750) are totally unnecessary. Changes of tonal texture, where appropriate, are often better achieved by slipping to a subsidiary manual division. However, in mature contrapuntal writing such as the great preludes and fugues of J. S. Bach, even changes of manual need to be carefully questioned, for the dropping and adding of contrapuntal voices (particularly in the pedal line) lends textural variation which sustains the listener's interest; dynamic changes of less than perfect subtlety can then be a distraction from the music. It should be remembered, however, that a decision not to change manuals must always be to a *musical* end, and that it may properly be taken only when the quality of sound is fine enough to attract the ear to the *music*, rather than to itself.

These principles also apply to later music written in classical style, or for performance on the instruments of Bach's day. Chief amongst such are the organ works of Mendelssohn, in which registration changes should be strictly limited, and used in intelligent association with the formal shape of the music.

With the advent of the later Romantic repertory, and the decline of the player's control over action and touch, changes of dynamic and of colour gradually assumed a greater importance. Simultaneously, increased technical demands upon the player's hands (arising from a more orchestral use of the instrument) meant that some form of assistance had to be provided, so that the organist could make rapid adjustments to dynamic level and colour during the course of the music.

At first such assistance was limited to the following.

1. A division of the organ which was totally enclosed in a box, one side of which resembled a venetian blind and could be opened and closed by a device operated by the player's foot (see Appendix, the Temple Church, London). Initially such a division was known as the *Swell*, but the system was gradually extended to other divisions, and by the 1930s entire organs were occasionally encased and 'under expression' (see Appendix II).

2. Ventils (operated by foot-pedals) which controlled the on/off supply of wind to certain stops on a manual or pedal division of the organ. This was a most useful method of preparing rapid changes of registration, and was a common feature of Cavaillé-Coll's organs (see Appendix, Ste. Clotilde, Paris).

3. Combination pedals operated by the feet, each pedal mechanically drawing a predetermined group of stops.

But with the advent first of pneumatic, then of electric servo-systems, press-buttons (*thumb-pistons*) were provided, usually under the keyboard of the division they served. At first the stop-combinations produced by each piston were predetermined by the organ-builder; later they became adjustable by the player, initially through the laborious system of selecting switches on a special panel, and finally by means of a convenient automatic 'capture' system.

In the performance of music requiring rapid stop changes, some form of mechanical assistance is appropriate. The alternative is to employ human assistants (often one on each side of the organist) to rearrange stops at the player's behest. This method may be companionable, but it relies heavily upon the registrants' musical instinct, mental reactions, and ability to remain calm under fire! The quality of performance is therefore no longer entirely under the control of the player.

As the contemporary organ renaissance gathers momentum, its more purist devotees sometimes view any form of mechanical aid to performance as detracting from the purity of the classical organ. If a particular instrument is intended solely for the performance of music written before 1750—perhaps specifically for music of a particular historic tradition—this attitude is entirely tenable, and arguably desirable; but in an organ intended also for the performance of Romantic and modern music, it is highly questionable. In respect of a concert hall instrument, where the requirements of simple 'theatre' demand that the player must be in full view of the audience, the total absence of aids constitutes an unnecessary pressure on the performer, detracting from his confidence and encouraging in the public the idea that the organ is an inflexible machine needing two or three people to operate it. The same principle applies to the church organist, particularly if he has to conduct his choir at the same time as he accompanies it on the organ; some form of assistance is vital if both are to be done efficiently.

It is perfectly possible today to combine full mechanical action (including stop-knobs) with a purely ancillary electronic system for the physical propulsion of the draw-stops. The argument that it is an undesirable and anachronistic aberration to introduce any electrical devices (save the blower) into a mechanical-action organ may be countered by the fact that an electrical failure in this system does not affect either the integrity or the working of the organ as a performing instrument;[10] indeed, such a system, by giving the performer confidence, increases the probability of more convincing musical performance, which must be, after all, the ultimate aim of the organ renaissance.

In the design of a new mechanical-action organ, some dialogue between the builder and the experienced performer can be of inestimable value in producing an instrument in which the physical barriers to musical performance are minimal.

The Tremulant

The organ's unflinching tones, while perfect for bold counterpoint and music of homophonic splendour, are not always ideally suited to the conveying of more gentle movement. In such music, the application of a subtle, wave-like motion, especially to long notes, can greatly assist the projection of musical line, as well as enhancing the music's appeal. 'Singing' and 'floating' have appeared hand in hand in literature throughout the ages.[11] Leopold Mozart, writing of vibrato on the violin, suggested that 'the Tremolo is an ornamentation which arises from Nature herself and which can be used charmingly on a long note, not only by good instrumentalists but also by clever singers. Nature herself is the instructress thereof. For if we strike a slack string or a bell sharply, we hear after the stroke a certain wave-like undulation (*ondeggiamento*) of the struck note. And this trembling after-sound is called tremolo, also tremulant'.[12] Geminiani, writing

---

[10] A purely mechanical 'capture-combination' system is possible, and exists on several modern organs in Europe.

[11] For example:

> My soul is an enchanted boat,
> Which, like a sleeping swan, doth float
> Upon the silver waves of thy sweet singing.
>
> (Percy Bysshe Shelley, *Prometheus Unbound*, 1819)

[12] *Versuch einer gründlichen Violinschule* (Augsburg, 1756)/ Eng. trans. by Edith Knocker, *A Treatise on the Fundamental Principles of Violin Playing* (Oxford University Press: London, 1948), ch. 11, p. 203. In a footnote added to the 1787 edition, Leopold Mozart clarifies his terminology: 'I do not mean

around 1745, was in favour of much vibrato on stringed instruments, but in flute music only on long notes. Leopold Mozart, however, felt that the violinist should be sparing—'performers there are who tremble consistently on each note as if they had the palsy'—and only use vibrato at places where nature herself would produce it, namely on 'a closing note or any other sustained note'. In music for wind instruments it seems indeed to have been generally felt that the sensitive use of some tremolo on long notes is desirable.

Certainly, in organ music, an induced vibrato, sensitively applied, can modify the organ's characteristic tones, making them float rather than pierce; though a continual, mindless tremolo, unconnected with the content of the music, can be a far greater distraction than steady tone. The tremolo (like the vibrato) must therefore be used only with discretion and conscious deliberation, having regard to the style and aesthetic pleadings of the music. Sometimes it may be vibrato which prompts the heart to flutter, sometimes its unexpected withdrawal. In music in which the tremulant might be generally in use, passages of stillness can sharpen the piquancy of suspensions or moments of chromatic tension, as illustrated in Ex. 2.1 from Bach's *Schmücke dich* (BWV 654). In short, the manner in which musical vibrato is used is yet another area where the performer's sensitivity, imagination, and good taste may be called into play.

Ex. 2.1

The Tremulant has been an integral feature of organ design for over three hundred years. At the time of the French classical organ, builders would incorporate both a strong and a gentle Tremulant (*Tremblant fort*, *Tremblant doux*), giving the player a choice according to the nature of the music and the type of sound being used: a gentle Tremulant was commonly used, for example, with the *Voix humaine*.[13]

Tremulant as it is used in organ-works, but an oscillation (Tremoleto)'. The latter refers to 'the remaining trembling sound of a struck string or bell [which] continues to sound not on one note only but sways first too high, then too low', and is the effect to be imitated on the violin. The organ Tremulant, by contrast, is less the product of fluctuations in pitch, and more the result of a varying *intensity* of sound; pitch alteration is a by-product, and is largely undesirable.

[13] In general, a faster vibrato is more suited to louder music. Cf. Leopold Mozart's *Versuch* on violin vibrato: 'the finger must move forward towards the bridge and backward again towards the scroll: in soft tone quite slowly, but in loud rather faster'. (ch. 5, para. 5, p. 98.)

During the nadir of the Romantic organ (the worst excesses of which were evident in the 1920s and 1930s), the Tremulant lost its identity as a truly artistic ancillary to musical performance, reflecting the contemporary custom of using vibrato in all forms of music-making; its constant presence was indeed an identifying characteristic of the theatre organ, and later of electronic organs in the field of popular music. When the pendulum swung to a renaissance of the classical organ, such widespread abuse resulted initially in a whole-hearted rejection of the Tremulant by many organ-builders, and it is only in recent years that a few have begun to devote serious attention to the problem of the organ's inflexible tone.

Modern experiments have focussed upon the methods of supplying and controlling wind entering the pipe-chests (rather than solely on the Tremulant), and they have yielded widely differing results. In the best instruments, the drawing of wind for successive notes or chords is allowed to create an attractive flexibility in its supply. In the hands of less successful builders, however, the control of wind can be so poorly devised that it is impossible to play a succession of rapid chords (e.g. the last ten bars of Bach's Prelude and Fugue in G, BWV 550) without causing violent fluctuations in the supply, or to perform a trio without hearing the movement of notes in one voice reflected in one long note held in another (e.g. the opening of Bach's Sonata II, BWV 526 (ii)). Inasmuch as it can confuse and offend the listener, such wanton unsteadiness of wind is artistically perverse; the origins of 'historical authenticity' sometimes claimed on its behalf constitute an insufficient reason for copying a system which arguably springs from unsuccessful technical endeavour, rather than from musical conviction.

A worthier ideal, offering more scope for musical development, may perhaps be found in an organ yielding a natural flexibility in the control of its wind supply ('free'—as opposed to 'unlicensed'—wind), combined with Tremulants designed to assist inconspicuously the projection of line, at the behest of the player; the addition of one *Tremblant fort* might encourage some interesting musical adventures.

If the Tremulant could be controlled always by a foot-pedal (for the hands are invariably occupied), the possibilities for its occasional use—on long notes, for instance—would be greatly increased; such a system exists on a few modern instruments, and is devoutly to be encouraged as a useful contribution to the organ's artistic flexibility.

Many different designs for the Tremulant have been developed over three centuries and more. It is for the organ-builder to decide—in relation to the style of his instrument—which design might be most musically suitable and even artistically challenging. Any matter connected with the winding of an organ must be an integral part of the instrument's design; it can rarely be successful as an afterthought.

3

A Basic Physical Approach to the Organ

Foot it featly, here and there

(Shakespeare, *The Tempest*)

THE mastery of any musical instrument requires a high degree of mental and physical co-ordination. For a keyboard player, the understanding and subsequent projection simultaneously of several lines of music, each with its own articulation and phrasing, adds to co-ordinative problems a dimension unknown to other performers. For the organist, who must often share several contrapuntal lines not only between ten fingers but with his feet as well, the degree of co-ordination required is greater than for any other musical performer (or indeed for any other occupation known to me).

In responding to such a challenge, the organist must learn to be an honest, self-critical listener; his own ear will be his best tutor, and its efficiency will improve with practice. However, first it might be helpful for him to consider several points of posture which are of basic importance to consistently good playing.

Balance and Posture

1. The organ bench should be at a height where the toe and heel can alternately touch the middle notes of the pedalboard without resting on it. Swinging the feet forward should bring the toes comfortably on to the front of the 'black' notes. The notes at either end of the pedalboard should be in reach of the toes with the ankles stretched.

2. An organist's feet are never on the ground! If not in use, the heels should be tucked back on to a bar joining the ends of the bench,[1] and if about to be used, they should be hovering near the pedals, much as the fingers almost touch the keys. He must therefore learn to balance his body so that he does not fall forwards. With practice, he can find a forward position on the bench which allows him to relax, and to swing his legs (from the knee) from side to side without falling on to the pedalboard or leaning backwards.

[1] On eighteenth- and nineteenth-century organs—notably those of Cavaillé-Coll—iron brackets, placed above the heads of the pedal keys, were sometimes provided as a resting place for out-of-work feet (see Dom Bédos' plate LII in Appendix I).

In relation to the manuals, the bench should be so placed that, with upper arms hanging relaxed and vertical from the shoulder, and the forearms extended horizontally, the fingers lie easily over the keys of the lowest manual. On many English organs of the last eighty years, the pedal 'black' notes will often feel further away from the player than is usual either on older or more modern instruments, while the lowest manual will be closer to his stomach. When in doubt, the most comfortable position of the arms and hands in relation to the principal keyboard (the Great or Hauptwerk) should preferably be the deciding factor.

3. Physical posture is of importance, particularly in the long term, because an awkward manner of sitting not only feels uncomfortable, but can also lead to spinal problems; the habit of sitting upright will pay dividends in later life. A simple experiment will explain the meaning of 'upright'. Sit erect on a hard chair and place the hands, palms upwards, beneath the bottom; in this position, one can feel the two protruding knobs of the pelvis. Then allow the body to slump, and the knobs will slide forwards as the spine curves. If one thinks of the knobs as the 'sitting base', the habit of sitting reasonably erect will soon be established.

Physical Symptoms of Nervous Tension

Most keyboard players experience, sooner or later, a sensation of tightness at the base of the neck and across the shoulders—an affliction which often strikes in the first few minutes of performance! The symptoms are associated with nervousness, are caused by poking the head forward and slightly hunching the shoulders, and can lead to referred tension in the arms and eventually in the fingers as well.

Muscles fall into two principal categories, postural (phasic) and dynamic (tonic). The properties of postural muscles are such that they are able to maintain a state of contraction for long periods without fatigue; this enables us to maintain a natural posture, such as standing upright. Dynamic muscles do not possess the same properties, and their function is one of quick action such as elbow flexion in lifting; once the action has been performed, the muscle returns to its state of relaxation until called upon to contract again.

The large muscle in which tension is felt across the shoulders (trapezius) is largely dynamic. However, if the player sits with his shoulders at all hunched, the trapezius is given a quasi-postural function, and the resulting tension due to fatigue of the muscle is gradually communicated to the arms.

So an upright and relaxed sitting posture can help in the player's battle with performing nerves. Remembering to drop the shoulders and not to poke the head forward is a good start. Before the performance, shrugging and relaxing the shoulders, in association with deep breathing, is a useful exercise: with the chin tucked in, hunch the shoulders and breathe in slowly, then breathe out and gradually drop the shoulders.

Through measures such as these, the undesirable physical symptoms of performing nerves may be kept at bay; the arms will remain relaxed, the fingers will be free to move with musical sensitivity, and tension may be transmuted to musical excitement.

Co-ordination and an Approach to the Keyboard

(a) A Centre of Reference

An organist often has a great deal to think about and to do; yet eventually all technical matters must recede into the background, leaving the trained subconscious to use relevant acquired skills in the service of one object only—musicmaking. It is therefore vital that he should be able to regard his hands and feet as an entity, and not as four wayward limbs struggling for a modicum of cohesion. The welding of hands and feet into an efficient and obedient implement is largely a matter of practice. However, a good frame of mind is also important, so that the limbs are, as it were, aware of their equal responsibility and their status in relation to their owner's demands. Let us look at one way in which this happy psychological state may be achieved.

Until a few hundred years ago, it was generally considered that the centre of the body (the stomach) was the seat of the passions. Certainly, in physiological terms, this was more logical than our contemporary use of the word 'heart' as a synonym for compassion and sensitivity, for the first physical symptoms of violent or passionate emotion are felt in the stomach, which 'turns over', as we say. Furthermore, man has been aware for at least two thousand years that 'the navel is naturally the exact centre of the body', and it is half a millenium since Leonardo da Vinci's famous illustration of the fact.[2]

During occasions of physical exercise in which the four limbs need concentrated co-ordination, I myself have found it psychologically useful to regard the

---

[2] *Vitruvius on Architecture*, Book 3, ch. 1, trans. F. Granger (Wm. Heinemann: London, 1931, vol. 1, p. 161). Classical Greek and Roman artists regarded the human body as the most perfect manifestation of beauty. In Book 3 of his great work, written probably between 31 and 27 BC, the Roman architect Vitruvius codified the proportions of various parts of the body; these proportions—summarized by the circle and square as illustrated by Leonardo *c.* 1487—were to be reflected in those of the temple, which 'must have an exact proportion worked out after the fashion of the members of a finely-shaped human body'. (p. 159.)

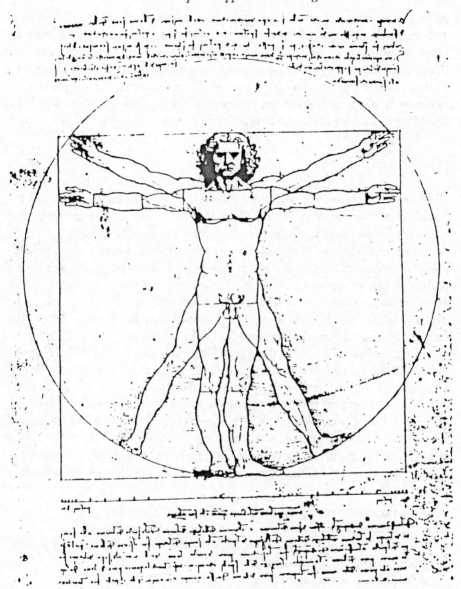

Vitruvian figure, Leonardo da Vinci. (By courtesy of the Accademia, Venice)

navel as 'the centre of operations'—the hub around which circles the wheel of activity. I believe this concept to be of considerable importance to the organist; when the limbs are called upon to be independent of each other (in the phrasing of contrapuntal lines), and yet simultaneously part of the whole musical person, a central point of reference can be both useful and reassuring. When playing the organ, as it happens, the natural position of the limbs in performance lends substance to the idea of the navel as a pivotal point.

(b) The Hands

Hands were not fashioned with the keyboard player in mind. In most cases the thumb and little finger are found to be too short, and the middle finger too long—admirable for gripping, but far from ideal for digital dexterity.

A simple experiment may illustrate the problem and demonstrate a possible solution, yielding the player the best possible use of all five fingers. Sit at a table—preferably one at elbow-height—and flex the right elbow to 90 degrees, then place the hand, palm downwards, on the table, with the fingers together; the disparity in the length of the fingers will immediately be apparent. Spread the fingers and thumb outwards, ensuring that the second finger is as close to the thumb as possible. Then twist the spread hand to the right until the tips of the thumb and little finger are equidistant from the edge of the table. It can then be seen that an imaginary line joining the tips of the thumb and little finger is more or less parallel with another one joining the tips of the second and third fingers. Imagine a line drawn back from the middle finger, through the hand, and onwards to the torso—where it will end up roughly at the navel, the central point of reference for the limbs. Now draw the fingers and thumb together until the nails of the second to fifth fingers are just invisible, and note the following incidental features:

1. the fingers are resting on their tips (NB *not* on the nails);
2. the fingertips form a shallow arc, and the hand is cupped;
3. the wrist is turned slightly inwards (and should be neither cocked upwards, nor hanging below the hand);
4. the forearm is near-horizontal;
5. the elbow drops naturally from the shoulder, neither being pressed against the body nor held outwards (which will cause tension);
6. the entire limb is relaxed.

As the fingers move up and down the keyboard, the forearm and hand should as far as possible remain in a straight line. The movements of the thumb or fingers passing under or over each other are a function of the fingers, and *not* of the hand, which should remain still. The principal movement of the hand is a lateral one, following the movement of the fingers on the keyboard.

In this connection, the fingers must be trained to stretch apart from each other. The factor which naturally restricts this movement is a lack of mobility in the soft tissues between the web-spaces of the fingers. Two simple exercises practised once a day before playing can be beneficial.

1. Place the tips of the five fingers together (one hand at a time) and hold the hand in front of the face as though examining the fingertips. Then with a rapid—though not violent—movement, throw the hand away from you, palm outwards, simultaneously stretching the fingers as far apart as possible. Hold this position for three seconds, and then return to a five-second study of the fingertips touching each other. Repeat no more than twice with each hand in turn.

2. With the forearm and hand in playing position, clench the fist for three seconds. Then, again rapidly, twist the wrist and simultaneously stretch open the hand, so that you are looking at the palm, but this time keep the fingers together, with the thumb at a natural angle of 45 degrees. Repeat no more than twice with each hand.

The fingers and hand should feel supple and well stretched. Remember that the essence of exercise is little and often, and that improvement takes time and cannot be rushed.

The physiological basis of all good keyboard playing is relaxed limbs, and, for the organist especially, the concentration of all sensitivity into the tips of the fingers. The player who 'expresses himself' in slow music by using his finger on the key as a pivot for his elbow to describe circles in the air is not only wasting energy, but is detracting from the sensitivity of his fingertips, and looking absurd into the bargain! Of course it is necessary (particularly in Romantic and modern music) for the elbow and forearm sometimes to make small lateral movements as the fingers are called upon to play large stretches, possibly at high speed; but the essential basic position should always be borne in mind.

(c) Approaching the Keyboard

At the end of the sixteenth century, the Italian musician Fra Girolamo Diruta wrote a comprehensive treatise 'on the true way of playing organs and quilled instruments', in the form of a question-and-answer dialogue.[3] A few extracts will show that his advice is as pertinent today as it was four hundred years ago.

[3] *Il transilvano* (in two parts, 1593 and 1609); excerpts in *Anthology of Early Keyboard Methods*, ed. and trans. Barbara Sachs and Barry Ife (Gamut Publications: Cambridge, 1981), pp. 35–6. Diruta was the only writer before 1750 to make a significant distinction between the touches appropriate to the harpsichord and the organ.

First, the organist must sit facing the middle of the keyboard. Second, he must not make gestures or movements with his person, but keep the body and head upright and grace-ful. Third, he must make sure the arm guides the hand, the hand staying in line with the arm; and neither should it be higher or lower than the arm—which will be achieved by raising the wrist to the point where the hand and arm become level. . . . Fourth, the fingers should be together on the keys, and therefore rather curved: in addition the hand should be light and supple over the keyboard, because otherwise the fingers cannot move with agility and promptness. And finally, the fingers must press rather than strike the key, lifting only as much as the key rises. . . .

. . . those who have poorly trained the hand appear crippled: they hold the arm so low that it is below the keyboard and the hands seem to hang on the keys . . . All this happens to them because the hand is not guided by the arm as it should be. . . .

. . . to cup the hand it is necessary to pull back the fingers somewhat, and so at the same time the hand is cupped and the fingers curved; . . .

To describe how to keep the hand light and supple over the keyboard . . . when one gives a slap in anger, great force is used. But when one means to caress and pet, as we do in fondling a child, one keeps the hand light, without using force. . . .

The effect [of pressing and striking the key] is this, that when the keys are pressed the harmony is smooth, whereas when struck it is choppy, as in the example below, of a singer who takes a breath for every note, in particular for minims and crotchets . . . making a crotchet rest between one note and the next.

It happens so to the unaware organist, who, by raising the hand and striking the keys, loses half of the harmony. Many fall into this error, and some thereby forfeit any hope of excellence; for when they want the organ to enter they place and remove their hands from the keyboard in a way which makes the organ remain without harmony for half a beat, and often a whole one, so that they seem to be playing quilled instruments, and to be about to begin some saltarello.[4]

To summarize the organist's playing position, it should be remembered that relaxed limbs, hand and forearm in a straight line, wrists prevented from rising, and a psychologically beneficial central point of reference are strong contribu-tory factors in confident musical performance. Above all, however, the fingers must always be well rounded. One must not play with the flat of the fingers, but neither should the click of nails be audible. J. N. Forkel relates that 'the holding

---

[4] Note that Diruta is here explaining legato as the form of touch most suited to the nature of the organ, and to the comparatively solemn music (much of it sacred) written for the instrument in his time. As may be seen in Chapter 5, the development of organ music in succeeding generations involves the use of comparative touches to achieve rhythm and accent, though these at no time negate the vital importance of legato in music-making (see p. 58).

of the fingers bent renders all their motions easy. There can therefore be none of the scrambling, thumping, and stumbling which is so common in persons who play with their fingers stretched out, or not sufficiently bent.'[5] This is a general principle, which is as important in music of the last two hundred years as it was in C. P. E. Bach's time, and that of his forebears. Flat fingers make flat music.

(d) The Feet

As vehicles for musical line, feet were surely even less in our Creator's mind than were a keyboardist's hands. The more remarkable is it, then, that at a time when the French used short pedals (sometimes only rods) for the cantus firmus or a slow-moving bass, and the English had no musical use for the feet at all, the feet of J. S. Bach were said by Ernst Gerber 'to imitate with perfect accuracy every theme, every passage that his hands had played. No appoggiatura, no mordent, no short trill was suffered to be lacking or even to meet the ear in less clean and rounded form. He used to make long double trills with both feet, while his hands were anything but idle.'[6] Indeed, this report of such pedalling prowess, though written some while after Bach's death, stands for all time as an artistic and technical ideal to which all students should aspire.

Much can be learnt from playing on pedalboards of this period, for their apparent limitations are a pointer to eighteenth-century posture and possible pedalling methods; they are also a reminder that the average height of today's man is several centimetres greater than that of his ancestor of 275 years ago—a point perhaps to be considered by the builders of modern 'classical' instruments. The early eighteenth-century player, so seated that his hands were comfortably placed on the lowest keyboard, would find that his feet, falling vertically from his knees, were resting on the pedalboard sharps—sometimes on their front edge, occasionally on the whole note. The naturals, therefore, could conveniently be played only with the toes, and as a further consequence, the player was forced to adopt a posture which was in fact very good for him: namely three right angles, at the 'sitting-base', knees, and ankles (Fig. 12(*a*)). On Romantic organs with longer

---

[5] *Über Johann Sebastian Bachs Leben, Kunst und Kunstwerke, von J. N. Forkel* (Leipzig 1802); trans. by 'Mr. Stephenson' and quoted in H. T.' David and A. Mendel, eds., *The Bach Reader: A Life of Johann Sebastian Bach in Letters and Documents* (Norton: New York, 1945), p. 308. Forkel (1749–1818), a professor at Göttingen University, based this essay on the life and works of J. S. Bach principally upon upon material gleaned from C. P. E. Bach and W. F. Bach, with some technical information from Quantz. The fact that he did not hestitate to give his own views does not detract unduly from an essentially meticulous report, presented in a highly readable form.

[6] *Historisch-Biographisches Lexicon der Tonkünstler* (Leipzig, 1790–2, Vol. I, columns 89–90), trans. in David and Mendel, eds., *The Bach Reader*, p. 263.

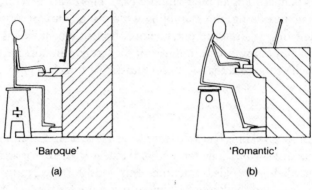

'Baroque'

(a)

'Romantic'

(b)

Fig. 12

natural pedal keys, and sharps placed further away from the player, the right angles are often distorted; also, it can be seen that the head and neck are encouraged into the 'poking' attitude described (and deplored) earlier (Fig. 12(*b*)).

The exact dimensions of early pedalboards differed from country to country and from builder to builder. Today, organs have a much more standardized pedalboard, though still with surprising variations in shape—flat and straight (the eighteenth-century German norm), flat and radiating, concave and straight, concave and radiating, etc.—and compass (from 25 or 27 notes for Bach and earlier—or one less, for bottom C♯ is often missing—to 30 notes in the second half of the nineteenth century, and occasionally 32 in the post-World War II era). Yet whatever shape is involved, the principles of good pedalling are the same now as they were in Bach's day, starting with posture.

The caricature of the organist with legs apart, elbows out, and arms akimbo resembles more the farmer sitting astride his tractor than a player attempting a musically elegant performance; and it is the potential clumsiness of the feet—compared with the hands—that is most likely to give rise to awkwardness, first of posture and subsequently of musical expression. So it must be one of the organist's primary aims to use his feet as though together they were to form a third hand; in functioning as a unit, the feet may achieve that physical elegance which forms a sound technical basis for the sensitive projection of musical line.

The variety of comparative touches available for the feet must be the same as for the hands (with which, after all, they are partners); the interpretation of a contrapuntal figure does not differ in the bass from how it appears in the treble, simply because on one occasion it is played by the fingers and on another by the feet! Legato pedalling is seldom impossible; on occasions when it is difficult, a solution sometimes involves the player in a closer *musical* look at the notes and the way in which they might fall naturally together into figures—lateral thinking which is no disadvantage in the interpretative process. This, after all, is the player's aim: a perfect fusion of technique and musicianship.

As with the hands, there is a psychological advantage in connecting the feet with a physical centre of reference; so once again we consider Leonardo's drawing (see p. 43). A few principles will outline the minimum technical basis. Sitting at an organ:

place the left and right toes on middle C and E (note that the modern standard for the position of the pedalboard in relation to the manuals is 'middle D beneath middle D', or occasionally 'D$^\sharp$ under D$^\sharp$');

keep the knees together, though not necessarily touching; imagine a line drawn from the toe of each foot through the back of the knee and on to the navel, thus providing yourself with that central point of reference which was earlier described for the hands;

play the pedals with the toes whenever possible. To this end, notes are depressed with a movement of the ankle, and the player should strive for an absolute minimum of up-and-down (or sideways) knee movement. The knees should be regarded purely as shock absorbers; it will then be found that instead of going *down* as a note is played, the knees will in fact often have a slight *upwards* motion. Using the heels entails a motion of the entire limb, which is tiring and decreases sensitivity of pedal touch;

note that the feet should stay as close together as possible. However, their combined width, side by side, is often greater than the width of two adjacent notes. Depending on the passage to be played (and the width of the feet), there are two possible ways around this problem: the notes can be played with the right side of the left toe, and the left side of the right toe; and one foot may be slightly behind the other. A combination of these techniques is often employed.

Hints on Clothing

Shoes are a problem! Many organists have at some stage tried playing without shoes, but this practice has two distinct disadvantages. A leather-soled shoe presents a flat (and relatively slippery) surface to the pedal key, allowing a greater subtlety of touch from note to note in advanced study; with unshod feet, I believe the opposite to be true. One also has the problem of whether to play (literally) with the toes or with the ball of the foot; the part in between can be quite tender, especially when up against the sharp edges of the 'black' notes. There is also the social problem of excusing the removing of one's shoes to the audience—does one walk on to the platform (or into the church) in stockinged feet?

It really is better to play wearing shoes. But whether one's feet are small or large, a few simple precautions will help to give the impression that there is practically nothing between them and the notes:

avoid shoes with welts around the sole;

choose thin, leather soles;

ensure that they are really pliable;

never wear them outdoors in wet weather, particularly before playing—or attempting to play—for wet soles will stick to the wooden keys and any thoughts of subtlety will yield to the urgent necessity of simply playing the right notes!

For the remainder of one's apparel, a little forethought can again be helpful in one's efforts to be relaxed and at ease on the organ. The organist must always remember that it is sometimes necessary to stretch a long way forwards, while not touching the bottom manual with the stomach[7] or allowing a jacket or cardigan to trail on to the keys. It is also necessary on occasion to stretch an arm sideways to draw a stop as quickly as possible. Inappropriate clothes can get in the way of such movements, and the main points to watch for may be summarized thus: ensure that your jacket or dress has sufficient give across the shoulders to enable you to stretch the arms forwards without straining the fabric or inhibiting your movements. If gentlemen can devise a form of dress that is smart, while avoiding a jacket, so much the better. Do not wear garments which have wide sleeves at the cuff,[8] or long, wide neckties. Trousers also should have plenty of room in their seat, and not have wide bottoms at the ankle. Trailing fabric can yield a sense of unease, though thankfully the passing of fashion has done away with trouser turn-ups, which were a constant source of irritation and an occasional embarrassment. The essence of good concert dress is that the player

[7] In the 1950s an English cathedral organist of extremely portly build had a contretemps with his head chorister prior to evensong. The boy also had the regular task of preparing his master's music and switching on the organ. Smarting from his rebuff, the boy determined on revenge. Drawing one of the electric-action stops for the lowest manual sufficiently for it to be 'alive', but not so far as to be immediately noticeable, he had his reward a few minutes later, for the arrival of the organist, sliding on to his organ bench, was heralded by a two-octave cascade of silvery flutes.

[8] Some years ago, when playing Bach's Sixth Sonata on a two-manual organ on which the keyboards were set rather closely together, the wide cuffs of my jacket were the source of near-disaster at bar 104 of the first movement. At that point the left hand is playing an upward scale of B minor, while the right hand is about to cross over the left and play middle F♯. With my right hand on the upper manual, it was only in the nick of time that I was aware of my left hand about to climb into my right cuff, trailing as it was on the lower keyboard.

should compliment his or her audience by having taken trouble (including taking into account local custom) and that the chosen apparel should be practical for the task in hand.

Good organists are formed from such basic features as those outlined in this chapter. To play well the performer must feel as one with his instrument. Technical ease is founded upon a comfortable demeanour, without which there will always be some degree of inhibition to impede fluent and expressive performance—the ultimate objective in any music-making.

4

The Technical Basis of
Movement and Expression

> The hands are a sort of feet, which serve us in our passage towards
> Heaven, curiously distinguished into joints and fingers, and fit to be
> applied to any thing which reason can imagine or desire.
>
> (Thomas Traherne)

THE increasing sensitivity of modern mechanical-action organs presents a
healthy challenge to the performer, for as well as conveying his musical intentions with greater fidelity, it can reveal his technical shortcomings in devastating
detail. The performer is therefore encouraged to apply himself not only to interpretative study, but also to the means whereby his interpretation may best be
projected to the listener. In matching his technique to the instrument's potential,
he is taking a vital step towards the ideal of the *interpretative entity* of performer-
and-instrument.

Some of the problems inherent in the organ as a musical instrument were
outlined in Chapter 1. The present chapter suggests a basic technical approach to
the instrument which, bearing these limitations in mind, will permit convincing
and effective music-making. It bears the same relationship to actual performance
as does a recipe to good cooking—only with constant practice and a good nose
might you turn out to be an Escoffier; only with a good ear and the intelligent
application of technique can the suggestions in this chapter be fully utilized. The
ear is the best organ an organist ever has, and often, alas, the least used; as with
any other part of our sensory apparatus, its capabilities will improve with
practice.

Pipe Speech

First we must examine the nature of the sound source that we are considering.
Quite apart from tonal design or general shape, the sound of an organ-pipe
contains three aural characteristics.

1. *Initial transients* (or random partials of the harmonic series). These are
produced as the wind strikes the upper lip of the pipe mouth. Their aural effect

can vary from a pronounced 'chiff' to little more than a clean, sharp edge to the note, comparable with the sound of the first letter in the word 'consonant'.

2. *The musical note itself*, the tone quality of which is dictated mainly by the design and shape of the pipe. The tone of the classical open (i.e. not stopped) pipe is characterized by an open, forward sound, comparable with the 'ah' contained in the first syllable of the word 'vowel' when it is pronounced slowly and deliberately. The tonal subtlety of a pipe is much affected by factors such as the type of wood, or the composition and thickness of the metal of which it is made. This is partly due to the density of the material used, since different materials yield different resonance characteristics and affect the development of harmonic partials.

3. *Resonance*. The body of a pipe resonates within itself; this resonance, combined with that of other pipes speaking simultaneously, is further qualified by the resonance of the organ's case and the instrument's general structure. When wind is cut off by releasing the key, the physical vibration of a pipe (its resonance) takes a fraction of a second to decay. This may be proved by placing one's ear close to the mouth of a Principal pipe while a friend depresses and releases the key; the most obvious results will be obtained from a 4′ pipe (tenor c on an 8′ rank) or larger. The decay of a pipe's resonance is comparable with the continuing ring of a harpsichord string *after* it is damped; and as with the harpsichord, such decay has a vital musical function which must be cultivated by the discerning player.

These three characteristics of pipe speech may be summarized as 'consonant', 'vowel', and 'decay', and the reader is urged to isolate them for himself at the earliest opportunity, choosing a Gedackt or Principal on a well-voiced organ, preferably in a fairly dry acoustical environment. Note that the consonant, as in speech, should not draw attention to itself by being very hard or over-extended, unless, as occasionally happens, 'chiff' is deliberately cultivated as a feature of the stop's character. Even large basses, such as the bottom octave of an 8′ Principal, should proceed directly to their vowel, via the consonant; an excessive transient time denotes poor pipe-making, or poor voicing, or a combination of both, though large pipes, by virtue of their volume, will take longer to speak than small ones.

Touch, Time, and Silence: The Techniques of Musical Projection

Musical expression is the manner in which musical content is communicated to the listener; but it is only a spontaneous device, and is no substitute for the composition of the music itself, or for interpretative techniques; effective expression can camouflage some of the music's deficiencies, but it cannot remove them. At certain times in the history of music, composers have tried to create a new style in which greater expressiveness is built into the notes. When expression springs from the player, the spontaneous robbing and paying-back of time has been loosely known for many centuries as tempo rubato. When the expression is a part of the music's construction, however, an intellectual and emotional understanding of the composer's intentions is needed, lest the music is *ab initio* wrongly performed. All musical performance calls for a blend of interpretation and spontaneous expressiveness, though the balance often shifts from one to the other, according to the style of the music. Two historic periods when the boundary between these aspects of performance became blurred may be seen in Italy in the early 1600s (discussed in Chapter 5) and in France some seventy-five years later (Chapter 7). For the moment, however, we are concerned only with the techniques of projection, and the possibilities for spontaneous expressiveness open to the organist.

The sound of an organ-pipe—unlike that of a piano—is unaffected by arm-weight: the volume and the tonal quality of a note is the same whether the key is pressed sharply or gently. Thus of the various techniques used by other musicians to shape line and phrase, those involving dynamics (whether to shape a whole phrase, to colour a particular note after it has been sounded, or to produce an accent) are not feasible on the organ. Phrases can only be shaped through a subtle use of the dimension of time. As we shall see, however, the possibilities for expression are much greater than they might seem to be at first sight.

'Tempo rubato' is a generic term meaning 'the alterations of time introduced by the performer for the sake of expression', and is a device 'as old as music itself'.[1] Nevertheless, its precise application has changed with the passing of the years, its one unchanging characteristic being that it must be spontaneous. So in order to avoid adding my readers to the infinite list of musicians totally confused by it, I shall use the term 'agogic accentuation' when referring to alterations of time within the pulse (mainly Baroque music) and 'rubato' when the alterations are within a musical phrase consisting of several pulses (principally post-Baroque, and mainly 'romantic', but see 'fantasy style' in Chapter 5).

The three main types of expression may be summarized as follows:

1. *Varying the comparative duration of notes in relation to each other* while playing in strict time. This is the principal Baroque method of accentuation by means of minuscule silences, and of shaping musical lines through the subtle use of *touch* to create light and shade.

---

[1] A. Dolmetsch, *The Interpretation of Music of the XVII and XVIII Centuries* (London, 1915), p. 284.

2. *Varying the duration of notes within each pulse (or beat)* so that attention is drawn to certain notes in particular, rather than to their neighbours (*agogic accentuation*, or *unequal notes*).
3. *Flexing the duration of consecutive pulses in an extended musical phrase*, within a disciplined time concept (rubato).

1. Silence and Comparative Touch

Varying the length of time that successive notes are actually sounded is a technique that may also be looked at via its corollary: varying the amount of *silence* between notes. The constructive use of silence in music-making is of vital significance in interpretation, for the effectiveness of musical sound is partly dependent on the quality and length of silence from which it emerges.

On all instruments other than the organ, the natural 'dying fall' of musical tone gives fresh impetus to the playing of each successive note. Thus, performers on quilled instruments must develop and cherish an effective legato technique, lest their musical lines lose continuity and become broken and choppy—though in the brilliant projection of fast passages (especially arpeggios) they have a built-in advantage over organists.

Conversely, the organist finds that passages requiring intelligent articulation—or simply the clean projection of consonants—must be carefully worked out in terms of a variety of possible touches; the sensitive combination of these compensates for the lack of inflexion in organ tone, creating the musical result most suited to the projection of a particular passage. Different touches in effect raise the question of minuscule silences in the context of the organ's continuous sound; these constitute the organist's principal means of phrasing, or of distinguishing note-figurations, or indeed of maintaining a lively forward-looking movement of contrapuntal line.

Silences are used in two ways:

1. to allow the consonant of the following note to be fully projected; this involves the purest and most subtle form of *détaché* touch, and is used to 'point' stressed notes;
2. as a *silence d'articulation* taken from the note preceding a musical figure; this is the equivalent of a breath taken by a woodwind player, and is the nearest approach that Baroque musical line makes to phrasing.

It is most important that these devices are distinguished one from the other in the player's mind, for though both involve silence, their musical *raisons d'être* are different: the first assists intelligibility in the projection of musical sentences, in the same way that clear consonants help an orator; the second breathes life and space into musical line, lending it fluency and elegance.

Thus it can be seen that the art of touch on the organ is not only concerned with the player's approach to the keys, but is also a matter of the relationship of successive notes to each other. What happens *between the notes* is of vital significance in the formation of phrases, and the considered *release* of notes is therefore just as important as a studied attack. Indeed, while a *pipe* has three parts to its speech, a musical *note* on the organ could be regarded as having five:

Pre-consideration (silence, or the placing of the note);
Consonant;
Vowel;
Decay;
Post-consideration (relationship with the next note).

(a) The Manner of Touch

Touch is the art of placing the fingers on successive keys in such a manner as will produce a considered musical effect.

The most common domestic instrument in use in Bach's time was the clavichord, perhaps the most sensitive keyboard instrument ever invented and the most difficult to play well. It is today still the best instrument on which the player can develop an almost sensual control of the fingertips while simultaneously being trained in the use of the ear, since it is so quiet. Many technical features of clavichord playing are directly transferable to the tracker organ, and before we launch upon a discussion of basic organ touch, let us consider what C. P. E. Bach has to say:

There are many who play stickily, as if they had glue between their fingers. Their touch is lethargic; they hold notes too long. Others in an attempt to correct this, leave the keys too soon, as if they burned. Both are wrong. Midway between these extremes is best.[2]

C. P. E. Bach does not then go into detail on this 'middle path', but Forkel is again helpful in the course of his reconstruction of J. S. Bach's manner of playing:

the five fingers are bent so that their points come into a straight line, and so fit the keys, ... that no single finger has to be drawn nearer when it is wanted, but every one is ready

---

[2] *Versuch über die wahre Art das Clavier zu spielen* (Berlin, 1753); trans. W. J. Mitchell as *Essay on the True Art of Playing Keyboard Instruments* (Eulenburg: London, 1974), p. 149. Hereafter cited as *Essay*. C. P. E. Bach's favourite instrument was the clavichord, and he saw clavichord touch as the basis for playing the harpsichord, pianoforte, and organ.

over the key which it may have to press down.... no finger must fall upon its key, or (as also often happens) be thrown on it,[3] but only needs to be *placed upon it with a certain consciousness of the internal power and command over the motion* [my italic].

Indeed, this thoughtful and deliberate placing of the fingers in due succession, each with its own touch as appropriate to the music's context, lies at the root of all good keyboard playing. The various touches available to the organist form a basic technical skill, and must be mastered if the music is to be convincing.

(b) Types of Touch

In all the explanations which follow, it is assumed that the reader is using, for his experiments, an organ containing a Principal (or Gedackt) that he can hear clearly, without the sound being diffused by distance or external resonance.

1. *Détaché*. This touch allows each successive pipe to sound all three of its speech characteristics before moving on to the next note. The right hand should be in the position described on p. 44, and should not move vertically during the scale, but only laterally as the fingers travel along the keyboard. Press each note with a gentle but firm and quick movement—do not allow the finger to rise unduly above the key, but keep it close, ready for renewed action.[4]

In this manner, proceed up the scale of C major (starting at middle C), allowing each finger to clear its note (i.e. allowing the pipe sound fully to decay) before the next is immediately placed. The gap (or silence) between the notes should be as small as possible, allowing only sufficient clearance between them *just* to hear the full consonant of the next pipe, and the next ... Remember that any unnecessary silence between the notes immediately interposes a personal or interpretative element into your playing, so that the effect created ceases to be that of pure *détaché*.

Having practised this technique, one can then proceed to a more advanced version of it. Instead of releasing each note by lifting the fingers vertically, the tip of the finger may be drawn gently back towards the palm, so that it glides off the end of the key in a caressing motion. The natural weight of the hand then drops the next finger on to its key in a manner that, with practice, yields clear articulation of

---

[3] David and Mendel, eds., *The Bach Reader*, p. 307. Perhaps Forkel has in mind the harpsichordist, whose fingers approach the keys in a different way, for 'quilled instruments want to be struck so that the jacks and quills work better' (Diruta, *Il transilvano*); though this is no excuse for violent movements of the hands.

[4] A similar technique is applied to the pedal keys; if they are *struck* by the toes, the resulting thumps and rattles can be most disturbing to the music. However, note that when playing chords with the hands and/or feet, it is sometimes advantageous to a co-ordinated attack for the keys to be struck from about 1 or 2 mm. above their surface, in order that the pallets may open sharply and simultaneously.

the scale. This technique is particularly useful in articulating rapid runs, as well as being of great assistance in the sensitive and pliant articulation of slow-moving lyrical passages. It was described by many writers, including Quantz,[5] but Forkel, in continuing his reconstruction of J. S. Bach's technique, finds perhaps the most poetic description of this elegant style: 'The drawing back of the tips of the fingers and the rapid communication, thereby effected, of the force of one finger to that following it produces the highest degree of *clearness* [my italic] in the expression of the single tones, so that every passage performed in this manner sounds brilliant, rolling, and round, as if each note were a pearl.' Remember, however, that Forkel is writing of the clavichord, and that the use of this technique on the organ is more limited because of the lack of natural inflexion in organ tone. Used with consideration and sensitivity, however, it is a most useful and musically effective manner of playing, akin to notes on a cello, each lovingly articulated with a separate movement of the bow.

2. *Legato*. This is traditionally the most prized of all performing techniques, because it encourages the maximum propagation of tone; that is, the vowel sound which, when variously pitched and inflected, conveys the emotional essence of music. It also happens to be the style of touch most suited to the organ's nature.

On a quilled instrument, by comparison, legato is so difficult to achieve that one writer after another has expounded the virtues of the organ: 'one can endow [the spinet] with no greater perfection than to allow its tones to sustain, like those of the viols or the organ' (Marin Mersenne);[6] 'on the organ one plays very legato. ... it has no need of all the devices that are used on the harpsichord [e.g. ornamentation] to compensate for the dryness of the instrument' (Saint-Lambert).[7] Indeed, as was seen in Chapter 1, the organist's problem is not how to achieve a continuum of tone, but the reverse: how to lighten the texture and allow it to breathe, while sustaining a singing continuity of line. If the harpsichordist's Achilles' heel is 'choppy' playing, the organist's equivalent is unremitting legato: of such is purgatory made! Nevertheless, as the ability to sustain tone is the organ's most characteristic asset, the player's command of a clean legato touch is essential.

In playing legato, we start by placing the fingers on the keyboard as before, over the notes C–G. Remember to keep the arm and hand fully relaxed, but the

---

[5] J. J. Quantz, *Versuch einer Anweisung die Flöte traversiere zu spielen* (Berlin, 1752; repr. Leipzig, 1906; facs. Cassell, 1953). Perhaps one may coin the term 'tip touch' for this useful manner of playing.

[6] *Harmonie universelle* (Paris, 1636). Mersenne (1588–1648) was a French theologian, philosopher, and theorist. His treatise is a prime source of information on contemporary musical instruments and on music and musicians at the beginning of the seventeenth century.

[7] Saint-Lambert, *Les Principes du clavecin* (Paris, 1702).

fingers filled with 'a certain consciousness of internal power'. This time we do not want to hear the consonant of each pipe (except for C), and in order to allay its effect we shall try to overlay the consonant with the decay of the preceding pipe. Thus we are endeavouring to place the vowel sounds side by side, touching but not overlapping. Having played the first note (C), lift the thumb cleanly, and simultaneously press the second with a quick, positive motion; and so on to G. While playing, listen to the relationship of each note to its neighbour: there should be no gap between them; a minimum consonant sound (or less than in *détaché*, anyway, depending on the type and quality of the action and the voicing of the pipes); no overlapping of the vowel sounds (i.e. two notes sounding at the same time); and thus a clean transition from each note to the next.

3. *Staccato*. This touch is employed chiefly for effect. Being essentially the most extreme form of *détaché*, it must be applied to musical line with great care. The player's approach to the keys is the same as for *détaché*, but the notes are released as soon as the pipes' vowel sound is established. Care must be taken not to make the notes so short that the listener hears only the consonant: the degree of staccato touch will therefore vary from organ to organ, according to the speed of the action and the way the pipes are voiced. Once again, the organist's ear is the only reliable arbiter.

(c) Touches as an Aid to Linear Momentum

First, it may be useful to remind ourselves of the constituent elements of music. *Melody* is a horizontal succession of single notes relying upon forward movement for its creation. *Harmony* may be thought of as a vertically ordered group of notes played simultaneously; it is a momentary aesthetic experience which, in the context of other moments implies forward movement through the play of tension and release in an overall scheme. The various dispositions of harmonic and melodic movement in the dimension of time yield *rhythmic interest*. When two or more melodic lines of equal importance are placed against (or 'counter') each other, the result is counterpoint. The essence of contrapuntal music is that the various lines interact in dialogue, during the course of which a harmonic pattern is revealed by the conjunction of the lines—which implies that the music must move, and be heard to move, constantly forward in a rhythmic (i.e. alive) manner.

The majority of the organ's finest repertory either is contrapuntal or has a strong contrapuntal element, and it is vital for the student to learn how to lead the ear forward, retaining the listener's involvement and curiosity as to the development and interplay of the lines which are being unfolded before him. A musical line cannot exist without movement, and the manner in which it moves (its rhythm) is an essential part of its life. The organist must appreciate that, for the listener (who does not have the advantage of his eye to clarify the perceptions of his ear), the *rhythmic projection* of a melodic line is a matter of the music's life or death.

The most effective way of projecting rhythmic groups of notes on the organ is by varying the duration—or sounding-time—of successive notes in such a way as to give aural substance to the natural idiomatic shape of the line. Such *articulation* depends upon the ear's ability to compare *détaché* with legato; if there is no legato, there can be no true articulation.

The musical phrase in Ex. 4.1 is shown first with deliberately exaggerated phrasing, marked in the conventional manner, and then in a form which can be explained in terms of silence, where 0 represents no break between the notes (legato); 1, pure *détaché*; 2, a minuscule silence; 3, a little more silence still . . . (4 would indicate a larger silence and 5 would mean staccato). In this example, consonants would be heard on c^1, f, a, b, and c^2. Note, however, that the musical context of f is different from that of c^2. The f is to be accented (or pointed) in order to show the rhythmic shape of the line, and to clarify the pulse structure.

Ex. 4.1

But c^2 is a cadence note, and this is indicated to the listener's ear by progressively shortening the preceding notes. The shorter the notes preceding a cadence, the more marked will be the final accent; but therein lies a trap for the unwary, for only a hair's breadth separates piquant effectiveness from unmusical caricature. In articulating musical line, the player is guided by musical considerations which are qualified only by the acoustical properties of the environment in which he is playing. Often the worst place to appreciate organ music is at the console; the organist must try to play always with the aural perceptions of his listeners in mind—his articulation clear, but subtle, and tuned to the room's acoustic.

2. Inequality and Agogic Accentuation

John Galsworthy observed a paradox of nature when expressing the thought that 'where Beauty was, nothing ever ran quite straight'.[8] However, one can only

---

[8] In the words of Jolyon: *In Chancery* (1920).

appreciate a curve by comparing it with a straight line, and so it is in music; one cannot 'bend' a succession of equal notes unless one first has the ability to play them strictly in time. So before discussing the bending of time, it is appropriate to observe the nature of the pulse.

(a) The Pulse Defined

In all music-making, a deep-rooted consciousness of the pulse (or 'beat') is the foundation of satisfying rhythmic movement. Indeed, the best parallel to a musical pulse is the human one. Regular movement of the heart is the first essential of human life, and so it is with music's pulse. An irregular or thumping heartbeat indicates a departure from the norm, and affects the life-process to a greater or lesser degree. An irregular or over-stressed musical pulse is likewise disturbing to the life-process of music.

The human heart, if it is to be healthy, must be respected; one acknowledges its importance through exercise and sensible diet and by avoiding excessive demands upon it. The musical pulse must likewise be respected, and in organ music, some gentle overt acknowledgement of its position is particularly important; for the impossibility of dynamic stress and the lack of tonal inflexion on the organ make the subtle marking or pointing of the pulse an integral feature of the music's rhythmic projection. The pointing is effected simply by 'clearing' the preceding note (through the subtle use of *détaché*) to produce a pipe-consonant on the pulse. In contrapuntal music, however, great care must be taken *neither to over-emphasize the pulse* (which would produce a 'thumping heart-beat') *nor to allow pulses to be acknowledged in all voices at the same time*. Simultaneous breaks in every voice damage that linearity which is the essential characteristic of good contrapuntal playing, and encourage a homophonic aspect detrimental to musical line. Overemphasis on the pulse, so that it seems to be forced upon the listener, likewise encourages a vertical aspect to the music.

Good reading of great poetry allows the words to flow within the gentle discipline of verbal accents; the listener is then only conscious of the logical unfolding of an experience, in which words and rhythm combine to create an aesthetic whole which transcends its technical parts. So with organ music: pipe-consonants are used to give intelligible shape to musical line, defining the pulse and lending the music rhythmic energy. But like all technical devices in music-making, this one must be used with subtlety, and always with good taste in the service of the music.

(b) Rhythmic Modification

If music were to be played with each note in its mathematically precise location, it would be an inconceivably boring exercise. Notation is an apparently accurate, though in reality extremely imprecise, way of committing musical ideas to posterity. In the process of realizing (or re-creating) the music, the performer constantly finds that certain notes are more important than others, and that the projection of a singing line involves numerous minute alterations to the length of notes in relation to their neighbours. But if the duration of notes were to be haphazardly modified without recourse to some disciplined structure, a musical line would soon lose its rhythm—and the listener's attention! The pulse, therefore, is regular and constant, though within its strict bounds lies the possibility of varying the length of its composite notes, irrespective of the touch employed.

There is little doubt that some form of expressive inequality in successive notes of equal value has existed in music ever since time and accent began to be formalized. The word 'Mū′sĭc' itself consists of one long and one short vowel, the metrical shape of which is underlined when set to musical notation. In instrumental music, which (unlike song) contains no natural accents, it is therefore only a small extension of formal metrical principles to regard certain notes as more important than others. Such importance can be conveyed by an accent achieved dynamically (which is impossible on the organ), or through the use of silences, or by *lengthening the duration of an important note in relation to that of its neighbours*.

Such extempore alterations to the length of certain notes may roughly be classified as (1) informal inequality; (2) formalized inequality; (3) other conventional alterations; (4) agogic accentuation (momentary expression).

1. *Informal inequality*. In 1565, the Spanish theorist Tomás de Santa Mariá was advising students that in 'playing stylishly . . . the way to play crotchets is to linger on the first and hurry the second . . . as if the first crotchet had a dot and the second were a quaver'.[9] He then gave examples of three ways of playing quavers unequally, while warning against the inelegance of excessive lingering (Ex. 4.2). The first is the same as for crotchets—a style 'used for pieces which are entirely contrapuntal, and for long and short passages of divisions . . . The second way is to hurry the first quaver and linger on the second'—'much more elegant than the first one.' The third—'the most elegant of all'—'is done by hurrying three quavers and lingering on the fourth.' This informal style was later assimilated by such composers as Frescobaldi, Purcell, and Handel.

---

[9] *Libro llamado arte de tañer fantasiá* (Valladolid, 1565), trans. Sachs and Ife *Anthology of Early Keyboard Methods*, pp. 7 ff.

Ex. 4.2

2. *Formalized inequality*. The basis of formalized inequality was laid down by Loys Bourgeois in 1550[10] when he linked inequality with time signatures (see Chapter 7), though it was to be another century before the subject was taken up and advanced by Guillaume Nivers, leading to the codification of *inégalité* in the great classical French school.

3. *Other conventional alterations*. In addition to inequality, certain other rhythmic conventions were understood and observed by composers and performers of the hundred years before Haydn. Those most commonly found by the organist are described below.

(*a*) Ex. 4.3, from Bach's Toccata, Adagio, and Fugue (BWV 564), and Ex. 4.4, from Buxtehude's 'Es ist das Heil' (BuxWV 186) demonstrate a convention which avoids dotting rests; and in this connection, the feeling that the smaller note of a dotted pair belongs more to the following accent than to its own group can often result in a dotted figure ♩ . ♪ being modified even as far as ♩.. ♪ .

Ex. 4.3

Ex. 4.4

(*b*) As a general rule, dotted-note groups sharpen towards a cadence. Ex. 4.5 shows the last bar of Buxtehude's prelude 'Gott der Vater' (BuxWV 190). It will incorporate a rallentando; as the pulses lengthen, the small notes continue at their previous length, thus effectively sharpening the dotted rhythm towards the final note.

---

[10] *Le droict chemin de musique* (Geneva, 1550).

Ex. 4.5

(*c*) In Ex. 4.6 from Bach's Sonata V (BWV 525) (ii), the final right-hand note probably matches the left hand, and becomes a demisemiquaver.

Ex. 4.6

(*d*) Where binary and ternary notation appear together (two against three), they are usually resolved in favour of the ternary, and either of the following:

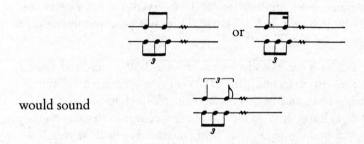

would sound

However, the organ's repertory includes a Bach prelude ('In dulci jubilo', BWV 608) which challenges the customary form of resolution. Bars 3–4 are notated as in Ex. 4.7, but in bar 25 Bach carefully notates some possible binary groups in threes (Ex. 4.8). The player may therefore wonder whether Bach might have intended the notation of Ex. 4.7 to be played literally, as written, in order to create deliberate rhythmic clashes (in the manner of joyfully clashing Christmas bells).

Ex. 4.7

Ex. 4.8

4. *Agogic accentuation*. The term 'agogic [i.e. attracting] accentuation' was coined by the nineteenth-century educationist Hugo Riemann to describe an expressive device in which the lengthening of a note produces an apparent accent.[11] In German (and later, American and English) writings its meaning was widened to embrace all expressive subtleties involving the modification of tempo, as opposed to stress accents obtained by dynamic means. The term proved to be of most value in the interpretation of organ music, in which, as dynamic stress is impossible, quantitative accenting has more immediate relevance and is indeed a most important means of expression. In recent years, however, its meaning has narrowed, and it is now most commonly used to refer to *the expressive shaping of line through subtle alterations to the composite notes of pulses moving at a constant tempo*. Such a definition is much to be encouraged, not least because it helps to distinguish quantitative variations within the pulse from the type of rhythmic elasticity found in rubato (see below). The term is therefore used most commonly in the interpretation of Baroque organ music.

The practice of lengthening an important note may usefully be regarded via its corollary: the shortening of notes of lesser import which surround it, to avoid the beat being too long and the pulse being pushed out of place. As a medium for learning the principles of this expressive device, the chorale preludes of Buxtehude may be strongly recommended. By marking the notes of the chorale melody, the student may quickly learn how to distinguish the effect of less important notes, thereby lending shape to the line. In Ex. 4.9, from Buxtehude's 'Komm, heiliger Geist, Herre Gott' (BuxWV 199), pointing is indicated by the sign ' and the chorale melody by — over the relevant notes. The third and fourth beats of bars 4 and 5 form ornamental groups, and the impact of the fourth pulse

Ex. 4.9

---

[11] *Musikalische Dynamik und Agogik* (1884).

in each bar should therefore be minimized: this may be a good reason to consider starting the trills on the note itself, instead of on the note above.[12] Throughout this exercise, beware of over-pointing the pulse, and consequently of making it 'thump'; the keyword must be 'subtlety'. . . .

The art of agogic accentuation can also be extended to create an illusion of varying tempo while in fact adhering to a strict pulse. An example of apparent accelerando may be seen in bar 20 of Bach's Fantasia and Fugue in G minor (BWV 542), where the pairs of demisemiquavers may be played progressively more quickly, the time gained in so doing being compensated for by progressively lengthening the semiquavers; added shape is lent to the phrase by slightly extending the opening of each pulse, as shown by my pause marks (Ex. 4.10).

Ex. 4.10

Thus it can be seen that the combined use of agogic accentuation, *silences d'articulation*, and pointing yields a powerful means of expression, particularly in slow organ music, where there is a greater need for expressive subtlety. For Baroque music of any instrumental genre, expressive techniques are a vital part of interpretative study; for the organist they are absolutely essential. Departing from the mathematical duration of note-values helps to create musical tension and beauty of line. In the words of a thoughtful eighteenth-century English musician, 'We may, perhaps, affirm with Truth, that *Inequality* makes a Part of the Character of Excellence: That something ought to be thrown into Shades, in order to make the Lights more striking. . . .'[13]

---

[12] Buxtehude's works contain several instances where a trill both played on the beat and begun on the ancillary (upper) note would result in ungrammatical (and ugly) harmony; e.g. the Prelude, Fugue and Ciacona (BuxWV 137), where consecutive octaves would be produced throughout the fugue:

German music of the early seventeenth century was in fact strongly influenced by Italian practice, in which long shakes—according to the context—could begin on the main note. Michael Praetorius (1571–1621), German musical scholar and composer, in the third volume of *Syntagma Musicum* (Wolfenbuttel, 1619) follows Diruta (*Il transilvano*) in suggesting a main-note interpretation for trills. If Buxtehude might have been influenced by this practice, albeit several decades later, the question must arise as to whether Bach—at least in music arguably influenced by Italian models—might occasionally have expected likewise. In this respect, Bach's approach to the long pedal trill (bars 178–84) in the Fugue of the Toccata and Fugue in D minor (BWV 538) is interesting and seems unequivocal.

[13] Charles Avison, *An Essay on Musical Expression* (London, 1752), p. 286. Avison (1709–70) was an organist, composer, and commentator on music.

3. Rubato

Agogic accentuation provides a means of attracting accents without altering the strict tempo of the pulse, while various forms and degrees of inequality in Baroque music lend grace and space in appropriate circumstances. These are suitable devices for lending flexibility to music that is based essentially on segmental ideas. But in music founded on longer sentences, its emotional appeal increased by a more spacious harmonic plan, a broader concept of flexibility is required; for the effect of agogic accentuation on a long melodic line might be the opposite of what was intended, breaking up the line rather than helping to float it irresistibly forward.

For around a century from about 1730, the term 'tempo rubato' was often used specifically to indicate rhythmic elasticity in an upper part, while the rhythm of the lower part was to remain unchanged. Thus, Daniel Türk (*Klavierschule*, 1789) described

the so-called *Tempo Rubato* . . . as being the last means employed by the player for the expression of his emotion and feeling. . . . One note is robbed of some of its value, and as much is given to another. A certain passage (*a*) being given, we have at (*b*) the *Tempo Rubato* through an anticipation, and at (*c*) through a retardation:

One can see from these examples that the length of the bar as a whole is not altered, . . . the time of the bass has not been disturbed, the notes of the melody only having been displaced. . . . This *Tempo Rubato* must be applied cautiously, for it might easily render the harmony faulty.[14]

This doctrine of the inexorable bass, to give it another common name, was one of the many devices used in the search for greater flexibility and expressiveness on the harpsichord and particularly the early piano. However, as the period of its principal use coincided with the organ's shrinking popularity, it need concern organists only in an academic sense; being intended mainly for solo-line music, it was in any case totally unsuited to the bulk of the organ repertory, which was founded upon contrapuntal writing. Of far greater importance to the organist is rubato in its wider and more liberated form, applied not just to one line, but to all composite parts of the music.

[14] Translation quoted from Dolmetsch, *The Interpretation of Music*.

Rubato exists to free music from aesthetic confines that might issue from the movement of the pulse or from insistent rhythms; it is the art of heightening music's effect by considering rhythmic flexibility as an integral part of the entire piece. The principal of good rubato (meaning 'robbed') is that the listener should be conscious of time not lost or gained, but simply stretched and relaxed: time temporarily robbed, though with every intention of paying it back![15] If this were to be done within the confines of a bar, the effect most often would be of restless, even erratic time-keeping. In Romantic music, however, there is a tendency for the ear to accept *the phrase* as a measure of movement, rather than short groups of notes based on the pulse. If, therefore, rubato is used *within the time-concept of a whole musical phrase*, it serves the structure of the music and can enhance its aesthetic. The progression from slower to faster and back again (the stretching and relaxing of time) is itself steady, and planned as part of the music's expression; at the end of a phrase to which rubato has been applied, the passage should have taken substantially the same length of time as if it had been played with no rubato at all. However, it is most important to remember that, if rubato is to be used at all, it is used not spasmodically, but consistently throughout the music: once introduced, it becomes part of the nature of that performance. Above all, it is used with subtlety, as a means to an end, and never for the means itself.

Thus it may be seen that rubato is not an excuse for unsteady rhythm and a loosely fluctuating pulse. As with all expressive devices, it will only succeed if it is based on the discipline of a highly respected pulse. There can be no true freedom without discipline: 'the more constraints one imposes, the more one frees oneself of the chains that shackle the spirit'.[16]

The difference between a musically average performance and one that is truly convincing could probably be measured in milliseconds of sound and silence. Even the most brilliant fingerwork executed at fantastic speed, while amazing the listener momentarily, will ultimately be of disservice to the music if the technical and aesthetic demands of line and expression are ignored. Music on the organ can be wrought as flexibly as on most other instruments; it just happens to be peculiarly problematic, demanding not (as many would have us believe) less musicianship on the part of the player, but infinitely more. In all this, a sensitive and discerning ear (that, as it were, of the listener) is the performer's best friend.

[15] 'A suggestion is communicated of "free time" but not "bad time"; "bent but not broken", as Matthay has put it, and thus, paradoxically, only a very good time-keeper can be a very good "rubatist" (if the word may be allowed).' (*The Oxford Companion to Music*, 8th edn., article on Rubato, P. A. Scholes; Oxford University Press: London, 1950.)

[16] Igor Stravinsky, *Poetics of Music* (Harvard University Press, 1946). In a 1986 press interview, the young jazz saxophonist Courtney Pine graphically conveyed the joy of playing with a deeply rhythmical drummer. It was 'like being in a big blanket, man. Support everywhere so that I was rhythmically free. Phew!—I've never felt like that before.'

5

Some Thoughts on Interpretation

'I should have more faith', he said; 'I ought to know by this time that
when a fact appears opposed to a long train of deductions it invariably
proves to be capable of bearing some other interpretation.'

(Conan Doyle, *The Valley of Fear*)

Introduction

(*a*) *Definitive Performance?*

If music were purely a science, how dull it would be! Imagine working out a
mathematical problem and demonstrating the answer, step by step, in public;
after a few 'performances', everyone would know the method and the conclu-
sion, and there would be no surprises left. In fact, surprise may be regarded as one
of the attractions of music-making: not in the vulgar sense of 'shock' or 'titilla-
tion', but in the revelation of the many subtle delights that lie strewn along the
contrapuntal paths of great music.

In seeking the 'best' interpretation, the performer is striving to re-create the
spirit of the music as perhaps it was first conceived by the composer, and to
project it to the listener in the most convincing manner of which he is capable.
To this end, it is important for him to consider the techniques and spirit of the
age in which the music was written. However, he would be unwise to try
slavishly to emulate a manner of performance *possibly* employed by the
composer, to the exclusion of his own educated musical instincts. For quite apart
from questions of technique, instruments, or environment, it must be said that
the creator's view of his own work is not ultimately definitive, nor is he
necessarily its 'best' performer; other musicians often find subtleties that the
composer himself had not been conscious of generating. Sometimes, indeed, it
can seem that the composer does not write as himself, but as a medium for the
Zeitgeist of his time; the spirit of the age speaks through him, and his agony is one
of comprehension and development.

Again, just as his contemporaries might have viewed a composer's music from
a different angle, so that process continues in the generations that follow; but

then, one must consider also the *Zeitgeist* that influences the new performer. As the popularity of composers waxes, wanes, and waxes again in succeeding generations, so the interpretative climate for a composer sees a shifting emphasis on one quality or another by successive interpreters and their audiences. One interpreter may come close to attaining a performance which is convincing to most of his audience; another might achieve a similar result by means of different emphases. One may therefore wonder which of them is the 'better' interpreter, and in asking reveal a phenomenon of our own *Zeitgeist*—that we tend to seek paradigms of excellence, and experts on whom we rely for instruction, not only on material things, but also on intangible matters of taste and the spirit. For a realization of its true potential, however, music relies on intelligent listeners: in terms of musical appreciation, the greater the listener's commitment and experience, the more likely will he be to appreciate the subtleties and surprises of performance. An answer to 'who is the better performer?' must therefore take into account the nature of the audience as well as the quality of the performer. But, assuming their audiences to be equally sophisticated, the probable answer will be that neither performer is 'better' than the other; for underlying the performance of each, and behind the various emphases of interpretation, is the supreme gift of music-making: the ability to convince listeners that this performance, at this point in time, in this place, conveys the essential spirit of this music. It is arguable that the ultimately definitive performance is a chimera; the best that an interpreter can do is to lend the performance real conviction for his own generation.

(b) The Dangers of Fashion

At the present time, there seems to be a strong belief that if we understand exactly how music was performed at the time of its conception, our performance—given technical proficiency—must automatically be good. This is not necessarily so. The performance might well be interesting, or even fascinating for a while, as we hear authentic instruments, or an expert in old fingering, or the latest advances into the pitfalls of *inégalité*; but all such scholarship is ultimately to no avail if the end-product lacks a genuine commitment to music-making. Musical scholarship is the servant of musical performance, but too often a 'rediscovered principle' is offered as the key that will unlock the mysteries of 'authentic' performance, when in truth it is but one facet of music-making to be considered by the thinking performer. Many good players who have taken aboard and applied the latest 'discovery' to the exclusion of broader musical considerations have ultimately regretted such a wilful departure from their previously balanced musical instinct.[1] So, while the performer must diligently study the facts that are there to assist his exploration of the music, the final responsibility for music-making is his alone. It is therefore of no musical consequence to a performer to be an expert on old fingering if he is unable convincingly to project a musical line; or to know more than anyone else about *inégalité* while being unable to sustain a rhythmic pulse. Rather must he study with an open mind, garnering facts, balancing argument and counter-argument, and always applying *musical* parameters to the latest interpretational fashions.

(c) Good Taste

The performance of French music during the reign of Louis XIV so abounded in unwritten customs that many French musicians wrote about their own national style with the object of persuading contemporary foreigners to play their music as it was meant to sound, and perhaps with an eye to posterity as well. In countless such treatises, one phrase constantly recurs, soaring above the minutiae of interpretation: above all the player is begged to develop and apply his *bon goût*. Without good taste, a performer can only partially be successful, and its application is as vital today as it was three hundred years ago. When considering alternative treatments of musical figures or questions of ornamentation, or when trying to establish an optimum tempo, or pondering a hundred other points, the player's instinct and good taste are often the only means of finally deciding the way that best serves the music. But first he must study, immerse himself in contemporary style, listen to other musical performers (particularly singers), and come to grips with the basic tenets of interpretation relating to his music-making. For instinct in most performers is a latent sense which has been developed from workaday experience, and *bon goût* must not be an excuse for idle scholarship; rather is it a fine polish, lending a beauteous sparkle to a disciplined, well-founded structure—and it can only develop through hard work and experience.

---

[1] This is by no means a modern phenomenon. Praetorius wrote in 1619 that 'There are many matters of this kind where the impression can be given that there is only one right way of doing something. So, for instance, some keyboard players are held in contempt for not using some particular fingering or other. This is ridiculous, in my opinion. If a player can fly up or down the keyboard, using the tips, mid-joints, or the backs of his fingers—yes, using his very nose if that helps—and either keeps or breaks every rule in existence, so what? If he plays well, and plays musically, it matters little by what means he does so.' (*De organographia*, Wolfenbüttel, 1619); Eng. trans. by David Z. Crookes, *Syntagma Musicum II: De Organographia Parts I and II* (Oxford University Press: Oxford 1986).

(d) Interpretation on the Organ

The art of interpretation, as it applies to the performance of organ music, is in many ways still in its infancy. For about a century from 1850, public attention was focused more upon the organ itself than upon the music written for it.

Since the early days of the organ renaissance, great strides have been taken by players and listeners alike in developing and appreciating interpretative skills in the context of the problems posed by the organ's unique nature. But the field is still bedevilled by partisan views and by varying technical and musical standards, so that the establishing of a consistent level of critical appreciation remains, by and large, a challenge for the future. Meanwhile, the task of the player is to study the techniques of interpreting music from the great periods of the past, and of projecting counterpoint with clarity and expressiveness; to apply such study with *bon goût* to the making of music on organs differing widely in tone and action; and to encourage the development of a strong repertory for the future, based on the organ's distinctive suitability for music of a primarily contrapuntal nature.

The French organ school of the *grand siècle*[2] is comparatively well documented with regard to interpretative techniques and registration; though the musical realization of those techniques is arguably more demanding of the player's powers of expression than is the interpretation of the music of Buxtehude and Bach, about which much less is known. This may partly explain why late twentieth-century musicians are concerned more with the interpretation of Bach than with the music of Bach's great French contemporaries. The highly stylized interpretative mannerisms of the *grand siècle* must be transformed into musical eloquence, and this process requires intense application on the part of the player. But for the music of Bach, interpretative guidelines are so scarce in comparison that there is infinite potential for argument over minutiae, and this can obscure the importance of musical expression, which is as important in Bach as it is in François Couperin. Thus, where the music of these two composers is performed by equally musical players, Bach tends often to be played with less musical conviction than Couperin, with the result that interpretations seem more open to argument. In my suggested approach to Bach playing (Chapter 6) I have therefore tried simply to outline a practical technical basis upon which a thoughtful regard for interpretation and projection might be built.

Before looking at these two great periods in more detail, however, let us consider some of the more important general characteristics of the period.

[2] This term is frequently used to define the golden age of the French classical school, though a more appropriate application would be to the seventeenth century alone, with sometimes the addition of Louis XIV's last years. It is nevertheless convenient and well-enough understood to be used in referring to the miraculous musical flowering that spanned a century from the mid-1600s.

Some Technical Considerations in Performing Baroque Organ Music

(a) *Musical Line*

It is one thing to talk of 'line' and quite another to achieve it successfully. For the keyboard player—and particularly the organist—a useful guide is to imagine the line being performed by someone whose music-making relies upon *breathing*—a woodwind player, for example, or a singer. In assuming that counterpoint contains the basic expressive features of song, the organist will at least begin the search for an expressive line in the right way. The principal considerations are:

1. breathing (in organ terms, *silences d'articulation*, which are used in the audible linear projection of phrases);
2. the effective use of consonants and vowels (which translates as touch and accent);
3. plasticity of line (agogic accentuation and other forms of inequality);
4. vocal colour (the use of registration to underline the aesthetic of a particular piece);
5. idiom (those interpretative features inherent in the realization of each composer's style).

'Above all, lose no opportunity to hear artistic singing. In so doing, the keyboardist will learn to think in terms of song. Indeed, it is a good practice to sing instrumental melodies in order to reach an understanding of their correct performance.'[3]

Technically speaking, line possesses two constituent features, each balancing the other:

1. a certain lift or lightness to the composite notes of the musical pulse, such as may be associated with the dance;
2. a consciousness of the irresistible momentum of successive pulses, grouped in a measured framework.

If either of these features is missing, the music can become a mere succession of (rather dull) events, and the performer resembles a man in a fog—peering only two steps ahead and unable to stride out with confidence. Music depends for its life upon movement, in the sense of a lively, continuous transition from note to note, figure to figure, section to section. It is an unfolding of one event in which many delightful moments play their momentary but cumulative parts in creating the aesthetic of the whole.

[3] C. P. E. Bach, *Essay*, Chapter 3.

(b) Fingering and Phrasing

In considering the niceties of convincing idiomatic performance, the player is immediately aware of the challenge of fingering; for one cannot accurately translate interpretative decisions into confidently projected musical lines unless the manner of fingering renders it possible. And in facing the challenge of ordering one's fingers, it is only a matter of time before questions of phrasing occur: should certain notes be grouped together, or not? This in turn involves the consideration of touch. Thus the various areas of interpretative techniques demonstrate their interdependence; when properly related, they form a basis for performing style. But without good fingering the player will never achieve the technical security that alone can give him the confidence to range his mind widely on matters of musical expression.

The purpose of any fingering method is to achieve fluency by presenting the fingers with the easiest and musically most effective way of performing a given sequence of notes. *Fingering must always serve interpretative decisions* —never vice versa!

'Which way is easiest and most effective?' is a question which has been argued and discussed for four centuries, though the most significant developments occurred in the two centuries before the mature works of J. S. Bach. There is no shortage of instruction books, from Hans Buchner's *Fundamentum* (*c.* 1520) to C. P. E. Bach's *Versuch über die wahre Art das Clavier zu spielen* (1753) and beyond, though examples of actual pieces of music containing indications of fingering are much more rare.

For most of this time, fingering was based on the use principally of the middle three fingers of each hand, with the occasional use of the thumb and little finger. All players observed the principle of fingering notes in pairs, which involved the crossing of fingers. The fact that they found no great difficulty in this method need not surprise today's student, who would find such fingering almost impossible on a modern keyboard; for three principal differences separate pre-Bach keyboardists from today's.

1. The music itself utilized a smaller compass (so that the hands had less far to travel to either end of the keyboard), and was comparatively sparing in its use of sharps and flats; the classical system of major and minor keys began seriously to be developed only in the latter part of the seventeenth century.[4]

---

[4] Though, by then, experimentation in the use of all possible tonalities had fascinated keyboard composers for about a century. John Bull (d. 1628) and his contemporaries were particularly adventurous: see Bull's Hexachord Fantasia, No. 17 in *Musica Britannica* 14 (Stainer and Bell, for the Royal Musical Association, 1951).

2. The natural keys were somewhat narrower and much shorter than modern ones—especially in the distance from the front edge of the naturals to the front of the black notes.

3. The player was encouraged to sit, at the harpsichord, facing slightly to his right, feet together, but with the right toe well out—a posture which greatly facilitates the crossing of fingers.[5] Such a position, however, would obviously have been impracticable for organists as the use of the pedals increased.

Girolamo Diruta, writing around 1600, was concerned specifically with the way in which an organist (as opposed to a quilled-instrument player) should approach the keys.[6] He was also the first writer to relate fingering to accents, proposing a theory of 'good' and 'bad' notes in which 'good' notes were played by 'good' (i.e. stronger) fingers. These were the second and fourth fingers of each hand, though he barred the use of the left-hand fourth finger in descending scales as it is weaker than the right-hand fourth (see Diruta's example in Ex. 5.1; the more usual left-hand descending fingering is shown, for comparison, in brackets).

Ex. 5.1

Other theorists from Spain and Italy imply a preference for the middle finger as the strongest one; from fingerings in virginal music it is clear that English and Netherlands players, from Byrd to Bull and Sweelinck, regarded the third (particularly in the right hand) and the thumb as the 'good' fingers. Santa Mariá fingered ornaments with 3 and 2 in either hand, thus influencing the choice of fingers in an ornamental passage.[7] Fingering in scale passages appears also to have varied with the speed of music.

Regardless of the choice of 'good' and 'bad' fingers, thumbs were used to facilitate the rapid movement of conjunct notes, and are not infrequently found, especially in the left hand. Short keys meant that the cupped hand covered a

---

[5] As it happens, this posture also enables the player to use the little finger of his left hand and the thumb of his right with greater ease, which is what Couperin may have had in mind in recommending it in *L'Art de toucher le clavecin* (Paris, 1716), p. 11.

[6] See Chapter 3.

[7] *Arte de tañer fantasiá* (1565). This treatise was also the first to discuss techniques of touch in some detail. The relative strength (and ease of control) of the second and third fingers is the best reason for always using them for ornamentation, where possible. The next best possibilities are the third and fourth, and the first (thumb) and third; the latter is particularly useful in trills which close with a black note, this being taken by the second finger.

greater compass than is possible on modern keyboards; this factor, combined with the position of the hand—the wrist being turned slightly inwards—meant that it was not unnatural or particularly awkward to use the thumb in this way. In Ex. 5.2, from Ammerbach,[8] notice also how the fingering of thirds stretches the hands at the sequences.

Ex. 5.2

The curiosity shown by keyboard composers such as John Bull and Sweelinck (1562–1621) in the use of remote keys was naturally complemented by ideas for fingering, some of which were unusual for their period. In particular, it is clear that all five fingers were used when the occasion demanded, though never to the exclusion of the principle of 'good' and 'bad' fingers. However, the transition from a paired-fingering system to one which consistently utilized all five fingers—replacing the crossing of the middle three fingers with a 'thumbs under' technique—was to be very gradual. Keyboard tutors using the old system were still being published when Bach was a young boy, and Bach even taught his eldest son to finger in the old way;[9] though by the time he was writing the first book of *Das wohltemperirte Clavier* (1722), his concern with remote keys and a new tuning temperament was necessarily being matched by new, logical ideas for fingering. It was not until 1739, however, that the first printed tutor to recommend exclusively modern fingering was published,[10] and another fifty years was to elapse before there was more or less general agreement that the middle fingers should not be crossed over or under each other.

Information on fingering used in France during the transition from the old system to the new is sparse and somewhat inconclusive, though some fingerings in André Raison's *Livre d'orgue* (1688) hint at the possibility of a connection

---

[8] *Orgel oder Instrument Tabulatur* (Leipzig, 1571). Elias Nikolaus Ammerbach was organist of the Thomaskirche, Leipzig, in 1561–95. J. S. Bach had a copy of the first edition of this work, which (from his annotations) he evidently found useful, probably as a teaching aid. Ammerbach's fingering system was well worked out and consistent. This musical quotation is taken from Sachs and Ife, edd., *Anthology of Early Keyboard Methods*, p. 58.

[9] He taught him so well, in fact, that Wilhelm Friedemann was reported (by Daniel Türk, *Klavierschule*, Leipzig and Halle, 1789) to have been able to play complicated passages with facility and at great speed, using only his middle three fingers.

[10] *Die Anfangs-Gründe des Generalbasses* (Leipzig, 1739), a treatise on figured bass by one of Bach's scholars at Leipzig, Lorenz Mizler van Kolof (1711–78). A year earlier, Mizler had founded the Society for the Musical Sciences, which Bach joined in 1747, and to which he presented the Canonic Variations on 'Vom Himmel hoch' (BWV 769).

between articulation and phrasing. However, all writers are concerned to stress fluency and grace as the prime essentials of keyboard playing, and an impression is given that the techniques of good fingering varied according to the aesthetic suggestions of their context. This is particularly the case in François Couperin's *L'Art de toucher le clavecin*, in which he discusses specific fingering for individual pieces, and includes modern ideas such as changing fingers on one held note (a device essential to good legato). But in reading his musical examples, such as Ex. 5.3, one must beware of assuming too strong a link between fingering and note-grouping, and of constructing principles of inequality (let alone of phrasing) where only a graceful style suitable for a specific piece was intended.

Ex. 5.3

There is no direct evidence from the entire period under discussion to show that a particular fingering implies any degree of phrasing. On the contrary, composers were concerned with the development of finger techniques that were 'easy, comfortable, graceful, skilful, and even'.[11] Conversely, however, the blind application of modern fingering to the passage in Ex. 5.3 would deny the music the intrinsic grace and character lent by the idiomatic fingering of its era.

Contemporary fingering techniques are a part of the interpretative background to the performance of music from this vast period, and detailed study can be both historically interesting and musically fruitful. However, by 1700 the whole question of fingering was in such a fluid state that it is wellnigh impossible to know how the composers of the high Baroque would have fingered their music.[12] It should be remembered, moreover, that modern performance must often to some extent be circumscribed by the limitations of the instrument at the player's disposal, and by its keyboard dimensions in particular.

The principles governing the choice of fingering may be summed up as follows.

1. Choose fingering which matches the music's articulative requirements, and plan the 'fingers over' and 'thumbs under' accordingly.
2. The hands should not move more than is necessary; be conscious of shifts in hand-position and try to manage them in such a way as to coincide with the demands of phrasing and articulation.

[11] Nivers, preface to *Livre d'orgue* (1667).
[12] See P. le Huray and J. Butt 'In search of Bach the Organist' in *Bach, Handel, Scarlatti*, ed. Peter Williams (Cambridge University Press: Cambridge, 1985).

3. Be awake to musical patterns or sequences which would utilize the same fingering.

Do not make any more fingering indications in the music than are strictly necessary (usually only 'thumbs under' and 'fingers over'): the fewer the indications, the more easily they are noticed, and the more precisely planned will hand-shifts be.

To phrase or not to phrase? The practice of indicating that a group of notes is to be considered as one articulative unit stems from music for voices or strings. In vocal music, the several notes belonging to one syllable form a natural articulative group; while in string music, notes contained within one movement of the bow are similarly grouped (and often marked with a slur). Such groupings are the essential nuclei of musical sentences, and can be of assistance to the keyboard player faced with questions of articulation. The combining of short sentences into long phrases, however, is a tradition not much more than a century old, before which the performer was expected to establish for himself the shape of musical lines and the manner in which linear momentum was to be maintained.

Baroque keyboard music rarely needs instructions as to the music's aesthetic, for the combination of recognized note-figurations, articulation, expressive conventions, and the underlying importance of the pulse will yield most of the 'directions' that a sensitive player could require. In Bach's organ works, slurs are rare; where they do occur, for example in his sonatas (which use a form associated at the time with stringed and woodwind instruments), they may draw the organist's attention to an articulative grouping of notes (or occasionally pulses) which, though natural for the player of another instrument, may be different from what by tradition might be expected in organ music.[13] Classical French composers employed conventions affecting both touch and inequality (see *notes inégale* in Chapter 7). However, although such instructions and customs might be regarded as the natural precursors of modern phrasing, they bear as little relationship to it as does the horse to the horsepower of an automobile. Both conventions seek to clarify stylistic method, but each in the context of its time.

For the organist, however, faced with the awful possibility of endless legato, and challenged by the need to propagate linear momentum, decisions about articulation nevertheless assume an importance undreamed of by a 'stringed keyboardist', whose notes are naturally inflected. Such decisions can come close

---

[13] But see Sonata II (ii), bar 5, and Sonata IV (iii), bar 3. Students are urged to avoid editions of organ music up to and including Mendelssohn which impose phrase-marks without indicating whether or not they are editorial. As a rough guide, any such music with phrases marked consistently over two or more pulses should be carefully investigated before use. Always choose an *Urtext* (original) edition if available.

to phrasing, so it is important in Baroque music for the organist to adhere to articulative principles as implied by notational figures and by the pulse. Additionally, he may reflect on the fact that conjunct notes (usually within each pulse) are viewed basically from a legato standpoint, while disjunct notes (as in arpeggiated groups) may be thought of literally as broken chords and viewed as candidates for *détaché*. However, it must be stressed that this basic guide is useful only as a starting-point, as exceptions to it are numerous. For example, the notes of a scale that immediately precede an accent may be played with some degree of *détaché* (especially in quick music) in order that the accent may receive its due impact; and instances will frequently be found where the occasional use of *détaché*—in juxtaposition with legato—can effectively increase the projection of a piquant slow phrase. Similarly, the first few notes of an arpeggiated phrase may well be less *détaché*—or even legato—in order to lend the line some initial momentum; and disjunct notes in slow music may well demand some application of legato if the line is not to sound disjointed.

Then there is the influence of tempo upon touch to be considered. 'In general the briskness of allegros is expressed by detached notes and the tenderness of adagios by broad, slurred notes', writes C. P. E. Bach, though adding, with the caution of experience, 'I use the expression, "in general", advisedly, for I am well aware that all kinds of execution may appear in any tempo.'[14]

In making decisions about touch, 'the best way' will usually yield a satisfying continuity (in the context of the music's aesthetic), together with that dash of lightness within the pulse and forward momentum that are so much part of lively musical line.

(c) Dialogue

1. *The placing of notes*. Contrapuntal dialogue should produce a musical aesthetic which transcends the sum of the individual lines: in this respect it may be compared with the productive result of a good conversation. It contains an element of drama, which is conveyed to the player in the characterization of the lines by motivic groups of notes; such drama is then expressed by the player through the rhetorical devices of enunciation, accent, and timing—or, in musical terms, articulation, pointing, and the placing of notes in the context of time. The use of articulation and pointing to achieve linear momentum has already been discussed; the new interpretative factor introduced by the consideration of drama is placing. This is the art of causing a strong note (e.g. on the pulse or half-pulse) to sound exactly on time, or apparently early, or apparently late.

[14] C. P. E. Bach, *Essay*, p. 149.

Placing may best be understood by thinking of the pulse as occurring not in the twinkling of an eye, but in a segment of time—however small. Greatly magnified, the principle is illustrated by Fig. 13, in which the blocks represent pulses, while the arrows show the exact moment that each note is played 'on the pulse'. Fig. 13(*a*) represents the pulse struck with mathematical precision—the normal way. In (*b*), the note is played on the leading edge of the pulse, in a manner which may be described as anticipating the beat. In (*c*), the note is on the pulse's trailing edge—minutely delayed. The contrast of (b) with (*a*) will create a sense of rhythmic urgency, while that of (*c*) with (*a*) will induce an air of pleasurable surprise, in effect stressing the importance of the delayed note. Such devices are the common stock of projection techniques, but, as with agogic accentuation and rubato, any deficiency in the player's pulse-keeping abilities will be magnified by any device which employs transient variations from strict time. Observance of the underlying pulse must be rock-like.

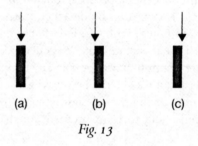

(a)   (b)   (c)

Fig. 13

2. *The projection of solo lines*: (i) *analysis and technique*. The dramatic implications of contrapuntal dialogue are perhaps best rehearsed in the process of learning to project such a line as the pedal solo from Bach's Toccata, Adagio, and Fugue (BWV 564) (see ex. 5.4). In this long solo, the working-out of musical argument is brought to life through the use of various degrees of *détaché*, the pointing of pulse notes, the imaginative placing of cadence notes, and the constructive use of silence. Remember that the pulse remains constant throughout (especially in silences), and note that the counter-statements (or echoes) do not require any alteration of registration; indeed, such a Romantic device would detract from the gravity of the argument, rather than assisting it. The sign – suggests a note of somewhat greater importance; + a note to be placed; ⌣ a slight yielding of movement (*cédez*).

In allegro solo lines (such as Ex. 5.4), the principal expressive devices are articulation, pointing, and placing; but in slow-moving lines, placing becomes

Ex. 5.4

less effective, and agogic accentuation is much more useful. A long coloratura-like solo, such as the passage in Ex. 5.5 from 'Nun komm der Heiden Heiland' (BWV 659), must be one of the supreme tests of a player's technical powers of expression on the organ, and it may be helpful to suggest three angles from which to approach such a challenge. The first requirement is to establish the pulse points, as shown by the brackets. Where these are crossed by a tie, the pointing should be heard at the beginning of the tied note; a note tied over the pulse implies a suspension, and pointing will focus the listener's attention and heighten the subsequent harmonic tension: in effect, the pulse's *accent* is displaced by one half-beat.

Ex. 5.5

The player's second task is to try to establish the harmonic progressions and the melodic outline around which the coloratura turns. A complex line such as this may well admit of different interpretations, but Ex. 5.6 is offered as a possibility. These notes may then be regarded as the structure around which a musical web is spun; if their significance is borne in mind, and the less important notes are moved on and 'thrown into Shades', the melodic outline will be able to lend the coloratura both melodic and rhythmic shape. In effect, one will be using the principle of agogic accentuation.

Thirdly, in terms of touch, the entire line may be played legato except for the pulse (or displaced-pulse) points, and those marked (i), (ii), and (iii):

at (i), the suspended tied note does not move directly to a resolution, and there should be a breath (*silence d'articulation*) between c² and e♭²;

at (ii), the four demisemiquavers are merely an ornamental way of proceeding from b♭¹ to g¹ and may therefore be detached from their immediate context to emphasize the importance of the main melodic notes; additionally, note that large intervals (such as b♭¹–g²) are seldom played legato;

at (iii) the g¹ has the effect of an anacrusis on to the b♭¹, and should be played rather short.

One of the characteristics of masterly composition is that all technical complexities tend to be subsumed in one expressive entity: though still requiring interpretative thought from the performer, the music is so logically presented that, compared with less mature musical writing, performance is relatively straightforward.[15] The corollary is that mature composition often contains hidden subtleties that the less experienced player may not be aware of, or may be unable to realize in performance.

The projection of solo lines: (ii) *the fantasy style*. By the first decade of the seventeenth century the polyphonic motet (with its complex points of imitation obscuring the text) was rapidly giving way to solo song accompanied by simple homophony, in which the text reverted to its former status as 'the master, not the servant, of the music'.[16] The text, once again, became the direct inspiration for the music's expression. The means of such expression in solo song (or 'madrigals') were first explained, with musical examples, by Giulio Caccini (*c*. 1545–1618) in the foreword to *Le nuove musiche* (1602).[17] This essay is important to *all*

---

[15] This is also the case with the listener's perception of performance—or indeed of an observer's perception of any practical skill: the more accomplished it is, the easier it appears to the onlooker.

[16] C. Monteverdi, *Scherzi Musicali*, 1607.

[17] This was the first published collection of songs in the new monodic style, and a landmark in the history of opera. An Eng. trans. of the foreword may be found in Oliver Strunk, *Source Readings in Music History* (Norton: New York, 1950), p. 377. The foreword is important also in its revelation of expres-

musicians because it explains the calculated spontaneity on which the style of the new music is based (and out of which opera was born). The foundation of the music is its harmonic underlay, the steady, simple progression of which gives security to the melodic and rhythmic complexities presented by the solo line.

In keyboard music, the revolution was hardly less dramatic. The sixteenth-century organ toccata which Merulo, for example, 'had treated in a form and style of imposing breadth and self-assurance' became in the hands of Frescobaldi a work which clearly illustrated 'the frenzied restlessness of the early Baroque period. ... disintegrated structure ... multiplicity of formations ... jerky motives, bold syncopations, and complicated cross rhythms'.[18] Girolamo Frescobaldi (1583–1643), in the Preface to the first volume of his organ toccatas (Rome, 1614), explains how they should be performed, noting that

the manner of playing with expressive passages and varied divisions ... must not be subject to time. We see the same thing done in modern madrigals, which, notwithstanding their difficulties, are rendered easier to sing, thanks to the variations of the time, which is beaten now slowly, now quickly, and even held in the air, according to the expression of the music, or the sense of the words.[19]

Frescobaldi is here insisting that the performer should add his personal dimension of freedom to musical lines which are already written 'expressively'. However, it would be an unwise performer who allowed his heart so to rule his head that all rhythmic shape and security were to be lost. Frescobaldi is seeking musical freedom, not anarchy, albeit with a high degree of rhythmic elasticity. It is a style that demands from the performer imagination, an underlying rhythmic integrity, and a strong commitment to Frescobaldi's expressed intentions.

Frescobaldi's pupil, the German organist J. J. Froberger, travelled widely (certainly to Italy, Austria, Germany, and England) and it is likely that the development of the *stilus fantasticus* in the north German organ school of Buxtehude and Bruhns owed a considerable debt to Froberger's influence.[20] The extended 'free' organ works of this period—variously termed 'toccata', 'prelude', and 'prelude and fugue'—were based on the idea of the canzona, in which a

---

sive rhythmic conventions in vocal music, which were no less complex than *notes inégale* in France later in the century; amongst Caccini's examples may be seen both *louré and coulé* figures.

[18] A. T. Davison and W. Apel, *Historical Anthology of Music* (Cumberlege: London; Vol. 1, 1947; Vol. 2, 1950). Commentary on Frescobaldi Toccata, Ex. 193. See also keyboard examples of Luis de Milan and Andrea Gabrieli in Vol. 1.

[19] The instruction is translated and commented upon in Dolmetsch, *The Interpretation of Music*, pp. 4 ff.

[20] Froberger (1616–67) was on terms of at least friendly respect with Matthias Weckmann (1619–74), a pupil of Heinrich Schütz, and of the influential Hamburg organist J. Praetorius (who himself had studied with Sweelinck).

section in duple time led to another based on similar material, but meta-morphosed into triple time.[21] The movements in strict counterpoint (*stilus canonicus*) in such works were linked by passages which were essentially extempore in character and which lent an air of fantasy to the entire work;

for this [fantasy] style is the freest and least restricted style which one can devise for composing, singing and playing . . . since one is restricted by neither words nor melody, but only harmony, so that the singers' or players' skill can be revealed . . . without close observation of the beat and pitch, though these do occur on paper . . . sometimes fast, sometimes slow; sometimes with one, sometimes with many voice parts; also sometimes a little behind the beat; without metre, yet not without a view to pleasing, to dazzling, and to astonishing .[22]

In bringing Frescobaldi's influence to northern Europe, Froberger's music contributes an organization of form and greater melodic and harmonic order. In losing some of the daring—often breathtaking—intensity of his master, Froberger gains a style which is perhaps more easily understood, the better thereby to be assimilated. Ex. 5.7 (the last four bars of Froberger's *Toccata II*) clearly demonstrates the kind of passage later to be found in the toccatas and preludes of Dieterich Buxtehude (1637–1707), Nikolaus Bruhns (*c.* 1665–97), and their contemporaries.

Ex. 5.7

---

[21] Bach, of course, provided the organ repertory with one supreme example of the canzona (BWV 588).

[22] Johann Mattheson, *Der vollkommene Kapellmeister* (Hamburg, 1739). Mattheson (1681–1764) was a German musician, composer, and important musical theorist. In this quotation, which is reminiscent of Frescobaldi's preface to his Toccatas (1614) quoted in this chapter, Mattheson's description of *stilus fantasticus* assumes something of the nature of the musical style itself; however, as was the case with Frescobaldi, his enthusiastic description of its free nature should not be taken to imply a complete lack of underlying rhythmic discipline.

Ex. 5.8

In Ex. 5.8 (a cadential coda from Buxtehude's Prelude and Fugue in F sharp minor, BuxWV 146), the musical challenge is perhaps to regard the first bar-and-a-half as a written-out accelerando, and the remaining half-bar as a rallentando to the cadence; the passage is an exercise in rubato—the two bars will take no more nor less time than if they had been played strictly as written.

The application of these principles may then be transferred to an interlude such as Ex. 5.9 (from the same work), in which the rhythmic interest of the line (four pulses to the bar) combines with harmonic movement (two in each bar) to produce a passage the freedom of which would be diminished by any marked relaxation of rhythmic discipline.

In Bach's organ works, the fantasy style is best exemplified in the Fantasia from the Fantasia and Fugue in G minor (BWV 542), in which fantasy and strictly contrapuntal passages alternate and interlink.

Ex. 5.9

3. *The projection of contrapuntal dialogue in trios*. The use of dialogue, seen in its most perfect form in the music of Bach, is a result of the mature combination of counterpoint and harmonic progression. In Ex. 5.10, from the third movement of Bach's Sonata VI (BWV 530), it takes the form of an animated conversation, in which two contrapuntal lines make a two-bar play upon the notes of a dominant seventh (on A), leading to another (on D), and returning eventually to the tonic

Ex. 5.10

(G). However, in the first movement of Sonata V in C (BWV 529; Ex. 5.11), an episodic discussion of a different kind takes place: instead of lines alternating in the manner of question and answer, establishing first one harmony and then another in a leisurely manner, we see a restless, closely knit argument which—such is the nature of discussion—produces change much more quickly; each successive bar starts in a different key, the harmony moving urgently from F to C to G to D until finally the principal theme appears in the relative minor.

Ex. 5.11

To the performer, each of these two types of dialogue calls for a different approach. Ex. 5.10 is the more stable, demanding performance in which the continuity and evenness of an unbroken succession of semiquavers is technically important; Ex. 5.11, however, contains an extremely strong motif counterpointing the semiquaver passage derived from the movement's second subject: the figure ⸓ ♫♪ conveys rhythmic strength,[23] while the following four quavers (involving strong intervals of a sixth) move the harmony irresistibly into the next key, and the next ... Such a combination of urgent rhythmic and harmonic movement marks the passage as one of cardinal importance in understanding the movement's character, and in deciding upon the optimum tempo. It is therefore vital that the player should achieve a lively, forward-looking air to the line, and the following analysis is offered as one way of projecting it convincingly.

The four quavers in the first bar of Ex. 5.11 each have a different role, though all four are played *détaché*: the first is a pulse note, and is pointed; it is also separated from the following quaver by an interval of a sixth, and is played medium *détaché*. The second quaver belongs in spirit to the third, and is a shorter note than the first; but the third is a pulse note (to be pointed), so c^1 and d^1 will not be played as a legato pair, but rather as two *détaché* notes, the d^1 perhaps rather longer than the c^1, as it is on the pulse. The fourth quaver leads to a cadence note and is fairly short, though not as brief as the cadence note itself. With practice, such analysis is much easier to achieve than it might appear at first sight; the object is always to propel the line forward through the use of comparative touches and varied note-lengths, according to the importance of each note relative to its neighbours.

4. *Dialogic devices in fugue*. The performing skills associated with dialogue lead one to consider the projection of a single line within a complex contrapuntal framework. For example, the clarification of a fugue subject in an inside part may sometimes be effected through the use of comparative touches in the various lines. In Ex. 5.12, from the Fugue of Bach's Fantasia and Fugue in G minor, one might wish to draw out the subject (which is in the tenor line); one way of doing this could be to reduce the amount of vowel sound in the alto and bass lines (bars 66–7) by playing them with a shorter touch, while giving more length to the vowel sounds of the subject.

From the listener's point of view, one of the attractive qualities of fugue is the recurrence of the subject in each of the voices. Inasmuch as anticipation is part of the delight in any pleasure, the performer may wish to give notice of an imminent entry of the subject, particularly if it is to occur in an inside part (alto or tenor). This he achieves by leading the listener's ear towards the entry through

---

[23] See Chapter 6, p. 95, for further discussion of this figure.

Ex. 5.12

the use of a mixture of touch (e.g. shortening notes prior to the entry) and agogic accentuation: even the slightest bending of the tempo around the point of entry will alert the listener's attention. In Ex. 5.13, from the 'Fugue sur les jeux d'anches' in François Couperin's *Messe pour les paroisses*, one may consider the following possibilities in preparing for the tenor voice entry in bar 47:

(i)   a very slight *cédez* (or yielding) of the crotchet preceding the entry;
(ii) the entry itself gives sufficient prominence to the pulse, and the bass line at * could be played legato;
(iii) as the alto line parallels the subject's first two notes, emphasis may be lent to the entry of the subject by shortening the alto a^1 preceding the entry point;
(iv) the subject must be in tempo; this may be emphasized by allowing the treble line's suspended a^2 to resolve on to g^2 very slightly late, thereby lending added harmonic interest at the entry point.

Ex. 5.13

5. *Lines with coinciding notes*. When the notes of one line coincide with longer or tied notes in another, C. P. E. Bach has some useful advice to offer,[24] not only

_____
[24] C. P. E. Bach, *Essay*, chapter 3, p. 159.

in respect of eighteenth-century music, but, as so often, for tonal music of later styles and periods as well. 'Occasionally', he writes, 'a short tie must be broken in order to clarify the leading of a voice (*a*) [see Ex. 5.14]. When in legato passages a voice is assigned to a tone directly after it has been taken by a held note, the hold should not be broken. Rather than violate the legato, the second tone's claim should be denied, for such notes are often written merely for the sake of notation (*b*). Should the two tones be well separated, the second must be struck, but in such a manner that the right hand will regain the key before the left hand has released it (*c*). If [however] the long note is trilled it must not be broken.

Ex. 5.14

When in doubt, choose a solution which allows the movement of the contrapuntal lines to be heard. This usually means giving precedence to the part which is moving, breaking the tie to repeat the note and re-establishing it from that point. In all such cases, the player should endeavour to preserve an overall legato movement—as implied by the existence of the long note or tie—using a subtle détaché touch to delineate the lines (see p. 57).

Summary of dialogue. An animated conversationalist exhibits thoughtfully disciplined views, listens with interest to the other voices, doesn't 'hog the floor', and expounds his arguments with life and vigour. A first-class string quartet can be a prime example of musical conversation (or dialogue), and a salutary lesson to the keyboard contrapuntist. For the organist, whose instrument is devoid of dynamic devices for expression, the cultivation of an ear sympathetic to the voices, and of fingers which accurately reflect those sympathies, is essential to enthralling performance.

Dialogue is at once the child of effective contrapuntal writing, and a pro-creator of movement. It could even be said to be the single most important stylistic factor in the interpretation of Baroque organ music, demanding a sense of dramatic effect and the insight and technical skill to use it to a convincing musical end. Because of the especial suitability of the organ for counterpoint, a proper respect for dialogue in the Baroque spills over into an awareness of dialogue and the importance of contrasting lines in the music of later generations. But the prime exponent was J. S. Bach, to whom we now turn our attention.

6

Towards a Grounding in Bach Interpretation

'Beauty is truth, truth beauty,—that is all
Ye know on earth, and all ye need to know.'

(John Keats, *Ode on a Grecian Urn*)

'You can only find truth with logic if you have already found truth
without it.'

(G. K. Chesterton, *The Man who was Orthodox*)

As a composer, no other musician has so thoroughly understood and responded to the organ's nature. Bach's handling of counterpoint fulfilled the instrument's musical potential and raised the art of organ music to a level comparable with that of any other instrument. Indeed, he set a standard which required his predecessors to be re-evaluated, and which illuminated for posterity the organ's potential as a musical medium.

Such great music demands the performer's closest attention to matters of construction, style, and interpretation, and it must be said that the latter will be a hollow exercise if it is undertaken without the complementary study of the way in which the music is constructed. Elegance, in part, springs from functional excellence which is in turn derived from architectural logic. In music, which depends upon interpretation for its ultimate expression, an understanding of the structure of the piece is therefore the basis of good performance; the performer who dwells upon the details of elegance without understanding the architecture of the whole will achieve only superficial communication. So the student is urged to become well acquainted with the music's structure first, so that his interpretation may be firmly rooted.

The characteristics of Bach's compositional idiom are such that his works invariably transcend their intended medium: many of his compositions (particularly those for keyboard) may be played on practically any other instrument or ensemble without damage to their musical essence—and they remain identifiably Bach. However, the corollary of this aspect of his music is that it can also be played with markedly different interpretative features without—to the casual listener at least—damage to its structure. Because of its inherently indestructible nature, there is a strong temptation just to play the notes, which in performance may then seem to be devoid of articulate metre, line, or subtlety. Perhaps this is a backhanded compliment to Bach's compositional style: the technical perfection of the music (often derogatorily described as 'mathematical') is seen as synonymous with its expression. The music is therefore presented archetypally, in an inexorable manner, and with flawless dexterity, producing either smooth, seamless counterpoint or a succession of single notes which resembles more the clatter of a typewriter than a singing line.

Nowhere else in the organ repertory is such a pragmatic aspect of interpretation so strong as in Bach's organ works, and there are as many different approaches to interpretation as there are schools in which the organ works are taught. Nevertheless, no musician dare lay claim to his interpretation being closest to the ideal,[1] for practically nothing is known of the manner in which Bach played his own music save that the results invariably enthralled his listeners. One can, however, point to certain stylistic characteristics and conventions of the period which may suggest lines of thought to be investigated by the player wishing to play Bach's works in such a way as to convince listeners of their unique musicality—as opposed to their purely technical perfection. Thus the pointers and suggestions which follow are intended to do no more than ardently encourage a thoughtful foundation upon which students may build a realization of their own potential.

Harmonic Structure

Among the most striking characteristics of Bach's music are its vitally strong harmonic basis and its well-developed sense of tonality. These underpin the play of shape and motif inside musical line: the interwoven lines are given a sense of direction and purpose through constant tension and resolution. As an illustration, we may compare Buxtehude's treatment of a cadence from 'Gelobet seist du, Jesu Christ' (BuxWV 189) (Ex. 6.1) with that of Bach (BWV 604) (Ex. 6.2). Note how Bach avoids a common chord resolution, keeping the ear in suspense

Ex. 6.1

---

[1] See remarks on definitive performance in Chapter 5 (Introduction).

Ex. 6.2

right up to the point where the next line of the chorale begins: his use of harmony thus contributes to the flow of the counterpoint.

In his setting of 'Durch Adams Fall' (BuxWV 183) (Ex. 6.3), Buxtehude's harmonic structure is essentially the same as that in Bach's setting (BWV 637) (Ex. 6.4). But in Bach's treatment, note how individual musical lines are moulded around this sound harmonic framework, enlivening it with linear momentum and a dynamic sense of continual expectancy. His use of chromaticism not only creates constant musical tension but also draws the listener into the drama of the hymn: it takes little imagination to hear God booting Adam out of the Garden of Eden with those great kicks of diminished sevenths.

But surely one of the greatest examples of continuous, mounting tension, each moment leading to yet another until the ear is inevitably led to the agony of Christ bearing 'our sins' overwhelming load', is in the final bars of 'O Mensch bewein'' (BWV 622), where Bach's compositional technique is fused with theological conviction in a pure expression of divine art (Ex. 6.5).

Ex. 6.3

Ex. 6.4

Ex. 6.5

I have chosen examples from the *Orgel-Büchlein* because one may see there the concentrated essence of techniques found elsewhere in Bach's work. The larger the form, the greater the need to determine the structural design of the music, so that its logic may be used as the basic foundation of our interpretation; starting with an appreciation of the structure, the interpreter proceeds to ever smaller details, so that figures and motifs become apparent as integral to the overall plan rather than decorative trifles superimposed upon it.

Bach's Musical Line

(a) Some Background

The story of musical line before Bach's time is one of constant endeavour towards longer phrases which, linked with others, allowed more scope for development: in short, a search for the key to a continual expectancy which would lead the ear constantly forward.

In the praeludium before Bach, generally speaking, short musical ideas produced short sections, in which musical interest was achieved by strong, rhythmical counterpoint. Contrasting sections (e.g. Prelude, Fugue 1, Fugue 2) were then linked together (often by interludes in the fantasy style), and bound tighter by such devices as motivic development and changes of metre from duple to triple, in the manner of the canzona.[2] As Bach's compositional technique matured, the short motifs of his predecessors developed into longer, more fluent lines, and the juxtaposition and interplay of these in contrapuntal dialogue encourage the ear to anticipate future musical moments.

[2] It is interesting to compare Bach's early Toccata and Fugue in E (BWV 566) with the Prelude and Fugue in E of Vincent Lübeck (1656–1740), and to examine Bach's probably even earlier Prelude and Fugue in A minor (BWV 551) in the knowledge that it was probably 'written before Buxtehude's manner had been fully understood and enlivened by [Bach]' (Spitta). See Peter Williams, *The Organ Music of J. S. Bach*, Vol. 1 (Cambridge University Press: Cambridge, 1980) for an interesting and scholarly account of both works.

In his 'free' works we see Bach's original genius for musical line at its most congenial. Mature fugue subjects, whether short or long, invariably lead into the countersubject with no audible join, but rather with an air of inquisitive curiosity as though looking over the immediate horizon to the next. It is this characteristic (which I have termed continual expectancy), in combination with a unique harmonic structure, that marks Bach's music immediately apart from that of his predecessors or contemporaries, and makes the study of the technique of linear progression so vital for the organ student.[3]

Parallel with the development of free composition in the organ repertory was that of the chorale prelude (as it came to be called), which had started life in the northern Europe of the early seventeenth century; simple, well-known tunes (sacred or secular) were varied and elaborated upon by such musicians as Sweelinck and his followers (much to the amusement of the populace, no doubt), in the same way that Dutch painters of the time drew inspiration from everyday scenes and objects. As the style grew, both in popularity and in compositional technique, two basic types of variation emerged—each of them capable of stylistic and technical development within its own form:

1. varying the melody over a simple harmonic or quasi-contrapuntal accompaniment (a technique in which Buxtehude excelled); or
2. using segmental ideas (often taken from the chorale tune itself) which were developed in a contrapuntal manner—a procedure especially favoured by Johann Pachelbel (1653–1706).

For Bach, the chorale prelude held a lifelong fascination. The combination of the discipline inherent in the use of a chorale melody, its harmonic and melodic possibilities, and the inner theological implications of the hymn to which it was set, was a constant technical and spiritual challenge. For students, the chorale preludes offer an insight into Bach's style unequalled by any of his work in other forms. As an excellent starting point for the study of line, one need look no further than the *Orgel-Büchlein*. Indeed, these forty-six preludes may be recommended as a lifelong source of discovery, inspiration, and refreshment in Bach's music.

[3] An interesting corollary to this study is that the techniques thus developed in relation to Bach can have a profoundly beneficial effect when applied to the problems of developing a cohesive whole from the various sections of, for instance, a praeludium by Buxtehude, Bruhns, or Lübeck. And after Bach, the study of line lends considerable understanding to one's approach to Romantic music; particularly, perhaps, to the interpretation of César Franck, some of whose organ music has elements reminiscent of the segmental style of the seventeenth-century north German praeludium.

(b) Characteristic Features of Bach's Musical Line

The use of certain rhythmic and melodic figures to propagate momentum was a strong feature of the period, and together with other Bachian features (such as polyphonic consistency and harmonic resourcefulness) may be seen in the music of many little-known composers of the period.[4] However, in the music of no other composer known to us are the techniques contributing to rhythmic impetus so fully worked out and sustained as in the music of J. S. Bach. For the organist (whose instrument contains so few naturally percussive or expressive elements), a working knowledge of the means by which Bach may be said to achieve rhythmic and melodic continuity of line is essential.

Of the many figures developed, I consider that two have an especial relevance to the style which Bach's music epitomizes. They are the *corta* and the *suspirans*.

1. The dancing *figura corta* is the most prominent. Sometimes represented as ♫ , it is most commonly found the other way round, as ♪ ♫ | ～ ; both forms may be seen in the C minor Fugue from Book 1 of *Das wohltemperierte Clavier* (Ex. 6.6). It is arguable that, to the average listener only superficially

Ex. 6.6

acquainted with the style, this fugue subject will be recognizable as at least 'sounding like Bach', its compelling rhythmic figure (shown in brackets) being largely responsible. Because the figure occupies half a pulse, the pulse itself is strongly emphasized by it; this emphasis (and hence the metrical structure of the work) is conveyed to the ear by 'clearing' the two semiquavers—in other words, leaving a knife-edge of silence before the pulse note. On the harpsichord (for which this fugue was written), the plucking of the strings and the consequent inflexion of the notes yields a natural articulation of the semiquavers; to achieve a comparable—or at least satisfactory—articulation on the organ, it might well be necessary to play the semiquavers considerably *détaché*, lest the phrase ♪♫♩

---

[4] The music of the Bohemian composer Jan Dismas Zelenka (1679–1745) is a strong example. Some of his contemporaries undoubtedly exerted considerable influence on Bach's development, among them J. G. Walther, who was a good friend.

should be heard by the listener as _y ♩ | _y and its rhythmic impact thereby be diminished.[5]

2. The *suspirans*, or 'breathing' figure, is so called because it starts with the sensation of a quick breath. Sometimes the 'breath' is literal, taking the form of a rest, though most commonly it is felt as a cadence note in the context of a line of running semiquavers. In Ex. 6.7, from Bach's 'Vom Himmel hoch' (BWV 606), both these contexts may be seen. Although the brackets in this extract are inserted simply to show where the *suspirans* occurs, they convey nevertheless an implication of phrasing (in the sense of a natural motivic grouping of the notes; phrasing in the modern sense is foreign to music of this and earlier periods). The

Ex. 6.7

passage and its continuation could be read as in Ex. 6.8, where a dot over a note indicates that it is played shorter than others in its immediate context.[6] In shortening such cadence notes, the player produces the sensation of a quick breath (*silence d'articulation*) which clarifies the following motif, and gives the line air and space. The combination of pointing and shortening a note in this way may be regarded as the organ's nearest approximation to stress accents on other instruments: it encourages intelligibility and helps to give the line rhythmic shape.[7] Note, however, that it must be subtly done, for the listener should be conscious not of breaks in the line (which would be detrimental to its momentum), but only of cleanly pointed and intelligently articulated counterpoint.

All other notes in Ex. 6.8 should be thought of basically as legato, though perhaps with the refinement of a touch which shortens slightly towards the next point.

---

[5] On the harpsichord, the desire for legato (and a consequently fuller sound) led sometimes to the deliberate overlapping of the notes forming the interval of a second. In his explanation of the *port de voix* (see Chapter 7), Rameau in 1724 shows ♪ ♩ _y . The influence on Bach of his foreign contemporaries is well known, and it is possible that such vocal effects in French keyboard music may have found favour in Bach's organ playing, to the extent of phrasing into the pulse or half-pulse; e.g. the 'spread chord' opening of 'Nun komm' der Heiden Heiland' (BWV 599) (see Peter Williams, *The Organ Music of J. S. Bach*, Vol. 3, p. 199).

[6] Cf. Walter Emery's edition of the *Orgel-Büchlein* (Novello: London, 1957), which retains the dots added by Ivor Atkins in the previous edition to indicate 'the release of the finger to show the end of the figure or phrase'. In my opinion these cadence indications are generally reliable and helpful to the student.

[7] Might this be what Bach had in mind when dotting and slurring the passage shown in Ex. 6.15?

Ex. 6.8

Analysis of Ex. 6.8

1. *Suspirans* and cadence note—the latter played fairly short in order to be cleared before the next *suspirans* starts.

2. Pulse-pointing, followed by the notes b and a played legato (a is not a pulse, and is diatonically conjunct with b).

3. Pointing and cadence note g, followed by a *suspirans* figure.

4. Pointing, followed by an unbroken group of semiquavers forming one whole beat and leading to a strong cadence.

5. Pointing of a *corta* in its less usual form. Note the strength of this figure, which is conveyed by its rhythmic nature, by the disjunct notes (which might well be played *détaché*), and by the dominant–tonic structure.

6. *Suspirans*. (Note that all *suspirans* figures should generally be followed by a pointed pulse note, thus preserving their essentially rhythmic function).

7. Pointings of both pulses and the last quaver of the bar, which is a displaced pulse (see p. 81).

We should remember that the *suspirans* figure was adopted and developed—not invented—by Bach, who often used it as the springboard for longer motifs more capable of sustaining line and encouraging momentum. One example among many may be seen in the countersubject of his Fugue on the Magnificat (BWV 733), where the *suspirans* gives rise to a constantly recurring motif (Ex. 6.9(*a*)). Possibly such a strong figure might be played without pointing the pulse note (f¹), especially as the pulse is so well marked in the subject (cf. the second subject in Sonata V (i), bars 51 and 52); the performer's task is to establish a good, sweeping momentum inspired by the motif as well as disciplined by the pulse.

Ex. 6.9(*a*)

On the other hand, simple scale passages might disguise figuration capable of making an elegant contribution to one's interpretation. In Ex. 6.9(*b*) (BWV 661)

Ex. 6.9(*b*)

the scales are made up of pairs of *suspirans*, one in the soprano line, the other in the alto.

(c) Analysis of Musical Line

1. *Cadence points*. The ability to analyse Bach's musical line is essential for the student, and the previous section has provided a useful introduction to this. As we saw in Ex. 6.8, a characteristic which lends impetus to a Bach line is the frequent occurrence of intermediate cadence points (often arising from the *suspirans*), so that the next phrase begins on the second semiquaver of a bar, rather than on the pulse itself: the little cadence point is at once the end of one phrase and a springboard into the next. Often, however, it is difficult to determine whether, for example, the first semiquaver is a cadence point or the beginning of a new group of semiquavers wholly contained within the pulse.

Consider the right-hand part in Ex. 6.10, an extract from Sonata V (BWV 529) (i). It starts with a *suspirans*, followed by a pointed pulse a^2. The question now is whether this note is to be played short (i.e. with the following notes played as a *suspirans* group) or legato with the other three (i.e. as the first note of a group of four). Before trying to resolve the question, let us look at the next bar: here, there is an obvious sequence, to be played as such, and this fact is underpinned by the presence of a hidden *corta* (B) which throws a strong accent on to the first of the sequential groups. The sequence is also preceded by a scale which may be played

Ex. 6.10

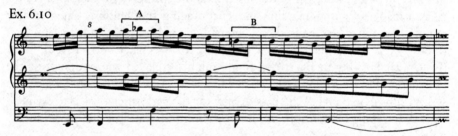

legato, though perhaps gently pointing the a^2 and d^2 at the beginning of each pulse. Reverting to the problem of the first beat of this bar, one may now see an alternative treatment, in which the figure at A could be regarded as another hidden *corta*; in that case, the first a^2 of the bar would be the first of a group of four semiquavers and the possible *suspirans* is ignored. This reading may be encouraged by the presence of the *corta* ⸻ in the left-hand part.

Whatever reading is eventually preferred, the prime consideration is to find the interpretation which best gives the line rhythmic momentum and which is musically convincing in the context of all three voices.

The difficulty experienced by players trying to determine whether or not a figure is in fact a *suspirans* may often be resolved by a quick rule-of-thumb check; Exx. 6.11 and 6.12, both from the Fugue of the Prelude and Fugue in B minor (BWV 544), provide instances. If the answer is to be 'yes', a group of three

Ex. 6.11

Ex. 6.12

conjunct quarter-pulse notes will usually appear in one of the following contexts:

(*a*) preceded by a quarter-pulse rest on the beat (A in Ex. 6.11);

(*b*) separated from the preceding cadence note by an interval of at least a third (B in Ex. 6.11);

(*c*) springing from the cadence of a group of notes of longer value (Ex. 6.12);

(*d*) following a clear cadence note, and constituting a change of direction (C in Ex. 6.11). This is the least positive identification of a *suspirans* figure, and must be treated with caution.[8]

2. *Suspensions*. In Ex. 6.10, the left hand has a suspended e² which resolves on to d² in the accepted manner. In such a case, the suspension must lead directly to its resolution: the relationship of e² to d² is legato, with no break between tension (suspension) and release (resolution). However, as may be seen in Ex. 6.13 (also from Sonata V (i)), tied notes may occur as part of a delayed suspension (A) or of no suspension at all (B). In these cases (and particularly where the tied note is a long one) the line will often be more clearly projected if the tied note is 'cleared' (i.e. treated like the cadence note preceding a *suspirans*) before the onset of the

Ex. 6.13

(L.H. part omitted)

---

[8] Long phrases derived from the sequential use of one figure can be unacceptably disrupted if the natural figurative articulation is rigorously applied. In this example from 'Erstanden ist' (BWV 628) the 'long view', with no cadence note until the a, will help the *suspirans* figures as they form a line which may be seen as symbolic of Resurrection:

next phrase. In Ex. 6.13 the principle is underlined by the presence of a hidden *corta* and cadence note (marked [·]) at the beginning of the sequential right-hand part.

In general, any tie followed by an interval of a third or more should be 'cleared' before the following note, though in all cases this principle must be qualified by reference to the underlying harmony. In bar 9 of Ex. 6.10, the left-hand tied f² should be followed by a breath: the whole bar is based on the dominant seventh, and the suspended f² is resolved by the right-hand eb² at the beginning of bar 10. Note that the left-hand motif in bar 9 (which is derived from the subject) starts on the second quaver of the bar, and so must anyway be separated from f² for that reason.

3. *Slurs and dots*. Bach used slurs infrequently in his organ music. The grouping of notes and any resulting phrasing stems from motifs and from the natural articulative process deriving from the pulse. Where slurs do occur, they may be indicative of articulative groups (as in string bowing), but do not necessarily imply an *all-legato* note-relationship, though the notes are felt to be connected. In the context of conjunct notes in a diatonic scale, perhaps the intention of a slur is to indicate a slight lengthening of the first note of the group (agogic accentuation); in Ex. 6.14 from Sonata III (BWV 527) (i), such a reading would underline the resolution of the suspension occurring one beat earlier.

Ex. 6.14

The significance of dots is not necessarily staccato, but an instruction to 'clear' that note before the next one starts. As we have seen, shortening the first note of a semiquaver group is one way of achieving an accent in organ music, being in effect an extension of the principle of the *silence d'articulation* (Ex. 6.8); the shorter the note, compared with its neighbours, the stronger the accent; the degree of shortness is therefore a matter of interpretative judgement. However, to think in terms of bowing will help to discourage the over-short touch (staccato), which can give rise to an exaggerated accent. Bach may well have had the violin in mind

Ex. 6.15

Ex. 6.16

anyway, as there are more slurs in the sonatas than in any other organ works. Ex. 6.15 shows an instance from Sonata VI (BWV 530) (iii); this may be compared with Ex. 6.16, an extract from Sonata IV (BWV 528) (i).[9]

Occasionally, Bach employs a slur which seems to indicate a departure from normal custom. For example, couplets are often played as such, as suggested in Ex. 6.17, from 'Puer natus' (BWV 603).[10]

Ex. 6.17

But in 'O Mensch bewein' (BWV 622), Bach gives a specific instruction to the contrary, giving the first B♭[2] a piquant significance by separating it from the demisemiquaver group, which in turn then sweeps the line towards the cadence (Ex. 6.18).

Ex. 6.18

Occasionally, a combination of the pulse and the way the notes are beamed might imply couplet movement in a scale passage, as in the alto line from 'Christe, aller Welt Trost' (BWV 670) (Ex. 6.19).

Ex. 6.19

The student wishing to study Bach's concept of articulative grouping in more detail can learn much from an examination of bowing-marks in the works for stringed instruments, and also to some degree from syllabic underlay (in the original German) in his vocal works.

[9] See Williams, *The Organ Music of J. S. Bach*, Vol. 3, pp. 203 ff. for a discussion of dots and slurs.
[10] See also Sonata VI (iii), bar 77. This figure is not to be confused with the often used 'sighing motif', e.g. (from 'O Lamm Gottes', BWV 618) 'useful in rising or falling form for situations requiring contrapuntal ingenuity' (Williams, *The Organ Music of J. S. Bach*, Vol. 2, p. 53). Nevertheless, it is difficult here to avoid the implication of a 'rocking' motif!

Rhythm, Pulse, and Tempo

(a) *The Momentum of the Quarter-Pulse*

Running through Bach's music is his pervasive use of apparently continuous quarter-pulse movement (i.e. semiquavers in 4-time),[11] not always in the one contrapuntal line, but shared between several lines so that a continuous movement is sensed in the music as a whole. It would seem that Bach intended such regular movement to be an integral part of his music's aesthetic; a good example from the organ works is 'Gelobet seist du, Jesu Christ' from the *Orgel-Büchlein*, in which, despite superficial appearances to the contrary, the four parts combine to sound every quarter-pulse in the entire work; bar 3 clearly demonstrates Bach's intention (see Ex. 6.2), through the precise, even fussy, way in which the music is notated.

It is a logical assumption that such unbroken movement requires consistent treatment, and the player's basic aim should be to create and preserve an underlying evenness and regularity. In Ex. 6.20, from Sonata I (BWV 525) (i), the semiquaver movement should basically be conceived as one continuous line, the pedal motif being accurately picked up from the second pulse note in the left hand.[12]

Ex. 6.20

conceived rhythmically as

This basic concept of regular movement is important in allowing the rhythm of the pulse and half-pulse to be more effectively projected; if the background movement is irregular, the listener's attention is drawn to that, and is deflected

---

[11] In puzzling contexts, the quarter-pulse may be read as the value of the smallest note consistently used in that piece.

[12] C. P. E. Bach writes: 'I know from experience that . . . short rests cause great ado among the most rhythmically sure and accomplished of other instrumentalists. All enter too late . . . Provided that he is certain of the tempo, his entrance will always be exactly right. Quantz in his Flute Method, p. 113, even advocates a delayed entrance (which goes to prove that a correct entrance is nearly impossible) and thus takes the lesser of two evils.' (Introduction to *Essay*, p. 32.)

from the rhythmic momentum contained within the contrapuntal dialogue. Of course, some contexts (particularly in slow music) demand a degree of flexibility in one's approach to the quarter-pulse; but such flexibility is itself disciplined by *motifs* and contained within the pulse. Flexibility is a musical attribute, but haphazard unevenness is more the product of lazy musicianship (see comments on agogic accentuation in Chapter 4).

(b) The Rhythmic Nature of the Half-pulse

The majority of Bach's works are written using notes in three principal time-values: the pulse, and the half- and quarter-pulses. In 4-time these are represented by crotchet, quaver, and semiquaver, and in 2-time by minim, crotchet, and quaver. The importance of the pulse and quarter-pulse has already been explained. Half-pulse notes are important in that they offer possibilities for more, or less, *rhythmic* projection according to the relative touches employed in a succession of them. In Ex. 6.21, from Sonata V (BWV 529) (i), the performer is

Ex. 6.21

looking for touch which encourages linear momentum. A simple experiment may show how small changes of comparative touch on the quavers can affect the momentum of the line in bar 2. The quavers should all be played *détaché*. The notes contained in the third beat should be basically legato, so that a² resolves on to its g² at the beginning of the next bar; the two semiquavers are ornamental in terms of the resolution and may be played lightly, shortening towards the pulse.

In our experiment, try playing the four quavers in the following ways:

(a) equal pure (i.e. long) *détaché*;
(b) equal short *détaché*;
(c) the first and third quavers long, and the others short;
(d) as in (c), but the fourth quaver shorter than the second.

In (a) and (b) there is little sensation of thrust in the line, because there is no way of marking the second pulse (e²), all the quavers being of equal length. In (c), e² and a² tend to be over-accentuated, producing heavy movement without the essential lightness of pulse essential to musical line. In (d), a medium-*détaché* first g² allows the pulse of e² to be gently pointed, while not overdoing it! The shorter second g² encourages the ear forward on to the third pulse and through it to the cadence; such a use of comparative touch binds the line together, giving it shape and substance. In the course of the experiment, notice the variety of movement produced by alterations of touch *only* on half-pulse notes.

(c) *Principal Pulses and Metre*

1. We are accustomed to think of the first beat of a bar as the most important one. This is a good starting-point, but in Baroque music bar-lines should never be regarded as 'iron bars', constricting the pulses into uniform groups. Perhaps the most common example of shifting main beats is the *hemiola* (the proportion of two to three, sometimes called 'sesquialtera'). Handel frequently used the device, notably at cadences, to which it adds a quality of firm resolution. In Ex. 6.22, an extract from the third movement of his Organ Concerto in B flat,

Ex. 6.22

Op. 4, No. 6, the duple stress of the pairs of 3/8 bars is changed to the triple stress of 3/4; notice how the harmonic patterns coincide with the changes in rhythmic emphasis. A particularly striking example of the *hemiola* in Bach's organ works may be seen at the end of the second section of the E flat fugue (BWV 552) from *Clavier-Übung*, Part III (Ex. 6.23). Shifting pulse patterns appear in numerous Bach organ works; in the opening passage of the Prelude and Fugue in G (BWV

Ex. 6.23

541) the pulses fall naturally first into threes, then twos (a sequential pattern), single beats, and finally two half-pulse groups leading into the cadence—an arrangement which creates mounting tension within a single line of notes (Ex. 6.24).

2. The performer often feels that music which is annotated in four pulses to the bar actually wants to move with a gentle underlying grouping of two in the

Ex. 6.24

bar, or, in 3/4, with a one-in-the-bar grouping; sometimes this is indicated, as in 4/4 by the time signature ₵. There can be two principal reasons for this phenomenon:

(*a*) melodic and/or rhythmic sequences which have the effect of combining pulses into groups (e.g. the principal subject of Sonata I (BWV 525) (i) Ex. 6.20);

(*b*) changes of harmony on the bar or half-bar instead of on every pulse.

Sometimes pulse-groupings can change in the course of the same piece. In the Prelude in E flat (BWV 552) the thirty-two-bar exposition is dominated by minim harmonic movement, while in the following episode, changes of harmony occur on the crotchet pulse; this alternation of emphasis, complicated by some crotchet movement on minim harmony, is then developed to intense dramatic effect.

The grouping of pulses is not always so obvious, and frequently amounts to little more than an 'aura' of double- or triple-pulse movement. However, as a general rule the player will find it useful to take a 'long view' of pulse-groupings in order to encourage linear momentum; but it must always be done with subtlety, and it must spring from suggestions within the music, rather than being arbitrarily imposed.

(*d*) *Tempo*

Tempo is an integral part of performance and must never be used as a means for display. All music has an optimum tempo, or an approximate speed at which performance is most effective. C. P. E. Bach recommends taking the fastest passagework into account to prevent hurrying. One can also usually find specific bars which, through some constructional or rhythmic feature, are more sensitive to and indicative of a certain tempo.[13] For an organist, the optimum tempo may be qualified to some degree by acoustic considerations, and possibly also by technical features such as slow pipe speech, or by the organ being buried in some far-flung corner of an echoing church. The test for the player is always what the listener perceives; a performance which at the console seems to be of virtuoso brilliance is as nothing in musical terms if the listener hears only a jumbled welter of notes.

Tempo must never be confused with rhythm. If one's performance of a Bach work sounds dull, the cause is more likely to lie in poor articulation than simply in a sluggish tempo. With every notch of speed faster than optimum tempo, articulation is less distinct, figuration becomes more difficult to project in an intelligible manner, and music-making gives way to note-rendering.

Rhythm may be thought of as liveliness. After a late night and oversleeping the next morning, one might have to run fast to catch the train to work, but one is probably feeling far from lively! Conversely, a good night's sleep and a leisurely breakfast followed by a gentle stroll will probably find one feeling very lively. So liveliness, while often reflected in physical movement, essentially stems from within and is not dependent upon speed except in connection with optimum tempo.

The Baroque allegro is particularly important in this respect: it moves with a cheerful liveliness, but is not very fast. Quantz's advice is apt: 'whatever rapidity the allegro may require, one must never go beyond a regular and reasonable movement.'[14] Most quick movements (often in *tempo ordinario*) in Bach's organ works are allegro unless otherwise indicated.

(e) A Note of Caution Regarding Articulation

Throughout this chapter, I have discussed matters impinging upon touch and articulation. The player must constantly beware of the dangers of over-articulation, and of a style of playing which in the desire for clarity of expression becomes fussy and disjointed. Understatement is invariably more effective than overstatement, and a subtlety of approach is more winning to the ear than stressing the obvious.

---

[13] See Sonata V (BWV 529) (i), bars 76–80; the beginning of this passage may be seen in Ex. 5.11. Such rhythmical dialogue loses its life if either laboured or taken too fast.

[14] J. J. Quantz, *Versuch einer Anweisung die Flöte traversiere zu spielen* (Berlin, 1752). Cf. C. P. E. Bach (*Essay*, p. 151): 'The pace of a composition, which is usually indicated by several well-known Italian expressions, is based on its general context as well as on the fastest notes and passages contained in it. Due consideration of these factors will prevent an allegro from being rushed and an adagio from being dragged.'

Also, one should remember that, on really fine musical organs, possessed of highly responsive action and well-voiced pipework, musically reasoned playing requires less consciousness of the various degrees of comparative touch. While the principles remain unchanged, the organ itself speaks with a more articulate voice, enabling the player to take a broader view of interpretation, and thus to give perhaps a more telling musical performance.

Such a brief guide to the nature of Bach's music, played upon the organ, can at best be only a starting-point for the student; it may seem detailed, yet of necessity infinitely more is left out than is included. I hope simply that enough has been said to encourage curiosity and exploration into a realm of wonder. At no age can one ever be satisfied, for the music of Bach transcends any exhaustive textbook explanation—or complete understanding by any one musician; were this not to be the case, its magic would diminish, together with the challenge, and its greatness would thereby be lessened. And it is the challenge which is the constant joy.

Hints on Ornamentation

Most contemporary advice on ornamentation in the eighteenth century was aimed at stringed keyboardists (clavichord and harpsichord), for embellishments of one sort or another are an important way of achieving not only stress and accent but also a pleasing continuity of line on an instrument on which legato is difficult. As we have seen, organists do not have this problem, and ornaments in seventeenth- and eighteenth-century organ music are comparatively rare. The organ's uninflected tones are indeed not best suited to ornamentation, and trills must be tackled with a good ear and a fine sense of touch, lest they interfere with the line rather than enhance it.

Despite writing for stringed keyboardists, C. P. E. Bach's advice is apt for any keyboard player. He advises the player, above all things to 'avoid a prodigal use of embellishments'; 'Regard them', he writes, 'as spices which may ruin the best dish or gewgaws which may deface the most perfect building.'[15] Ornaments should marry with the music which they embellish, so that the listener hears them as an

---

[15] *Essay*, p. 81. C. P. E. Bach may well be cautioning the player to resist the temptation to sprinkle snappy little attention-seekers on the face of the music. Excessive extra embellishment is a constant threat to the clear expression of contrapuntal line, and often arises from the player's inability to achieve satisfactory communication through more subtle means; just as it became a notorious practice in C. P. E. Bach's time, so in this late twentieth century is it showing signs once again of encroaching on interpretative practice in organ performance.

integral part of the music's aesthetic.[16] To this end, they should be rehearsed with the same loving attention that is given to the principal notes of the music, and should never be regarded as mere 'extras' to be fitted in at a later stage; technical considerations aside, the interpretation of apparently identical ornaments may vary in detail from one to another according to their musical context and the general shape and flow of line.

With regard to the execution of ornaments, remember that the fingers should be curled, the tips staying close to the keys and not lifted high away from them, so that minimum physical movement is required to achieve an even, crisp legato. The arm and hand must always be completely relaxed, with energy concentrated in the fingers alone.[17]

Interpretation of the ornaments used in J. S. Bach's organ works is based on an *Explication* which appears, in Bach's own hand, at the beginning of the *Clavier-Büchlein* written for his eldest son, Wilhelm Freidemann, in 1720. This is the only word left by Bach on the matter of ornamentation. It is not an exhaustive list and leaves in the air the question of whether Bach altered his performance practice between 1720 and 1750; nor does Bach relate the ornaments to musical contexts. Nevertheless, even though the *Explication* is only a simple guide written for a ten-year-old boy being taught by his father, the modern student will find no better foundation upon which to build his study of Bach's ornamentation. It is shown in Ex. 6.25 (the numbering is mine).

In studying the *Explication*, two basic rules may be assumed:

1. ornaments *begin on the beat*, with the exception of the *Nachschlag* (see below), which is not included in the *Explication*;
2. the notes of ornaments conform to the key of their immediate context.

Trills (shakes) are indicated by the sign *tr* or ⌴. The number of strokes in the latter should not be taken to indicate the number of repercussions in the trill, the length of which depends principally on its musical context: a short ⌴ can sometimes indicate a long trill. They should always be played with a sufficient number of repercussions to indicate that they are in fact ornamental. At the same time, the speed of trills should be compatible with the mood of the music: an abrupt or 'snappy' trill would usually be out of place in a slow, lyrical movement, while too little speed in an allegro could cause the repercussions to confuse the melodic outline of the music.

---

[16] Lectures on ornamentation by the late Thurston Dart in the early 1950s were enlivened by apt aphorisms on the blackboard, one of which was 'when in doubt, leave it oubt'; nevertheless, this should not be read as an excuse for idleness!

[17] See p. 44 ff.

Ex. 6.25

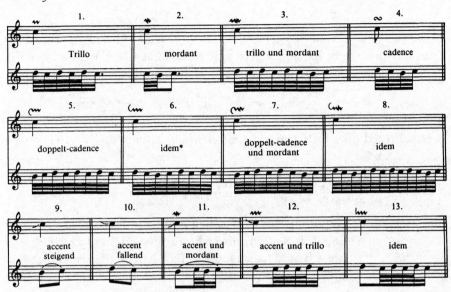

* meaning 'the same' as the previous one.

As shown in the *Explication*, trills begin on the upper (or auxiliary) note, unless this results in ungrammatical harmony such as consecutive octaves or fifths. However, there is enough evidence to throw doubt on the absolute inviolability of such a rule, and students should certainly acquaint themselves with the relevant arguments. A good starting-point is Walter Emery's *Bach's Ornaments* (Novello: London, 1953), pp. 38 ff. Emery quotes four kinds of short shakes that are described in eighteenth-century writings, of which, in the following example, the first two begin on the auxiliary (upper) note, and the other two on the main note. His explanatory paragraph is worth quoting:

No. 1 of the Explication is a Trillo, and no. 12 shows a slightly prolonged Imperfect Shake combined with an appoggiatura; thus, these two forms of short shake are authenticated. Bach undoubtedly used the Schneller also, and most probably the Pralltriller; but players should be a little cautious with these two forms: with the latter because there is no absolute proof that Bach used it, and with the former because there is a tendency to use it too often, at the expense of the Trillo.[18]

---

[18] p. 69 ff. Material reproduced by kind permission of the publisher.

Trillo

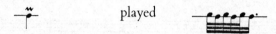

Pralltriller (may only be used where the second beat is defined by a note in another part, so that the tie can be distinguished)

Schneller (used only in fast music and on strong accents, and is often played staccato)

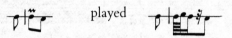

Imperfect Shake (appearing on a weak part of the beat and incorporated into the line in a legato manner; this ornament is akin to *tremoletti* of pre-Classical Italian music, which start on the main note of the trill)

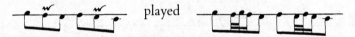

With that in mind, it may be seen that in Ex. 6.26(*a*) from Sonata I(i), a *trillo* is unlikely: as the pulse is the crotchet, and the ornament is on a weak part of the beat, a *trillo* would disturb the flow of the melodic outline and give undue emphasis to what is essentially a passing-note (Ex. 6.26(*b*)). A *Pralltriller* cannot be used, as there is no moving part under the trill-note to clarify the tie. So, as shown in Ex. 6.26(*c*) or (*d*), the best result might be obtained from an imperfect shake, played legato to the B♭. (See also footnote 12 on p. 66).

The *Explication* demonstrates trills with closing notes in Nos. 3, 7 and 8. Bach shows only an abrupt ending to the *trillo*, though closing notes were not only

Ex. 6.26

allowed but were often expected where the context was appropriate, even when they were not indicated in the sign. When interpreting the *trillo*, the player must therefore use his judgement as to whether or not closing notes improve the shape or flow of the musical line. They seem customarily to have been used at the end of long trills, and C. P. E. Bach's explanations go some way towards classifying other suitable contexts. In general, an abrupt ending emphasizes an accent on the following beat, whereas closing notes smooth the transition from the trill to the next beat, thereby lessening its impact.

In dotted groups, closing notes are often written in; where they are not, the trill should generally stop on the dot.

Closing notes in rhythmic figures such as 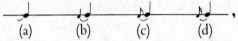 form part of the ornament and may be played faster or slower than the note-values indicate, if thought appropriate, according to the mood of the context.

The appoggiatura (or accent) (Nos. 9 and 10 in the *Explication*) may be written in any one of the following ways, which are identical in meaning:

(a) occasionally appears as a double hook ℧, but this does not alter the ornament's performance;

(b) usually appears in association with a minim ;

(c) and (d) seem to be interchangeable, and neither should be taken necessarily to imply an appoggiatura of that particular value.

Appoggiaturas are played on the beat. Their length, taken as a proportion of the main note's value, is a challenge to the musical judgement of the player, based on the following principal considerations.

1. A discord, apparent or implied, is regarded as more important than a concord and therefore receives the longer accent. Quantz states the rule that

when there is a shake on a note that is discordant with the bass—an augmented fourth, diminished fifth, seventh, or second—the appoggiatura before the shake must be quite short, so that the discord shall not be turned into a concord. For instance, if the appoggiatura a′ [in the following Example] were held half as long as the following ♯g′, on which there is a shake, one would hear a sixth (f″ to a′) instead of a seventh (f″ to g′); that is to say, there would be no discord.[19]

---

[19] *Versuch*, quoted in Emery, *Bach's Ornaments*, pp. 78–9.

2. It is possible for the appoggiatura to take up to half the value of the main note (or up to two-thirds of a dotted note). However, Emery suggests that, in learning a new piece, all appoggiaturas should at first be played short, 'at the very most a quarter of the main note, or a sixth if the main note is dotted. Later, one should experiment with longer intepretations, giving due attention to consistency.'[20]

3. Appoggiaturas are sometimes used by Bach in association with a *trillo* (Nos. 12 and 13 in the *Explication*), and, as can be seen, imply a gentle lengthening of the auxiliary note. Bach's note-values in the *Explication* add up to more than a crotchet, and whether he meant

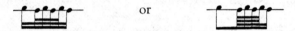   or

is an open question; but the principle is clear, and the amount of lengthening of the auxiliary note is a matter for the player in a given context, bearing Quantz's rule in mind.

The *Nachschlag* (or *passing appoggiatura*, as it is sometimes known) is not included in Bach's *Explication*. It is written using hooks or small notes in exactly the same way as the appoggiatura; distinguishing the two ornaments is therefore most important, for whereas the appoggiatura is played on the beat, the *Nachschlag* is played *between* the notes of descending thirds (cf. the French *port de voix*; see p. 129). However, not all descending thirds imply *Nachschläge*; as Emery points out, when comparing bars 12 and 23 of Meine Seele (BWV 648; Ex. 6.27(*a*) and (*b*)), it would seem likely that the small notes in (*b*) are appoggiaturas. In the passage from 'Allein Gott' (BWV 662), quoted in Ex. 6.28(*a*), the first three hooks are likely to be *Nachschläge*, while the fourth is an appoggiatura; Ex. 6.28(*b*) shows a possible interpretation.

Ex. 6.27

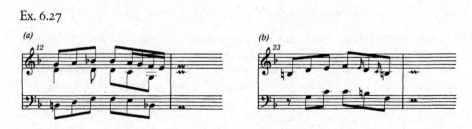

(a)   *(b)*

<hr />

[20] *Bach's Ornaments*, pp. 79–80.

Ex. 6.28

Sometimes one's interpretation of an apparent appoggiatura has to be modified through its later use in a different harmonic context; for example, at the beginning of the second half of the slow movement in Bach's Sonata VI (BWV 530), we see what appears to be an appoggiatura, beginning on the beat (Ex. 6.29(*a*)). However, when Bach proceeds to the repeat of this section, it is apparent that an appoggiatura would produce ungrammatical consecutive fifths. The ornament (which occurs in a descending third, as it happens) would therefore be better played as a *Nachschlag* (probably on both occasions, if one is to be consistent), as shown in Ex. 6.29(*b*).

Ex. 6.29

Ex. 6.30

The slide is generally played on the beat, as in Ex. 6.30, from the slow movement of Sonata III (BWV 527).

The Mordent[21] (No. 2 in the *Explication*) may be played exactly as Bach wrote it, or with a greater number of repercussions

---

[21] This spelling is usual today, though Bach wrote the word differently.

It can also appear in association with an appoggiatura, in which case it might be played as

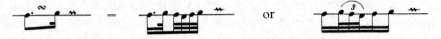

Note that mordents generally occur either on main beats approached by leap, or in a rising scale passage. It is rare to find them in a descending scale, and similar ornaments in such a context are more likely to be a form of imperfect trill, as explained above.

The cadence (or turn) is usually played briskly, though it may be played more gently in slow movements. It consists basically of a turn around the indicated note, either by sounding the note itself first

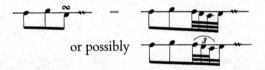

or by literally turning around the main note, as in

or possibly

This account of the principal ornaments found in Bach's organ works is intended only as a résumé, and further detailed study and practical experience is strongly recommended.

Hints on the Registration of Bach, his Contemporaries, and his Immediate Predecessors

Bach's specifications for the reconstruction in 1709 of the organ at St Blasius, Mühlhausen, are the best technical indication of his thinking on organ sound that we have (see Appendix). However, he left Mühlhausen before the work was undertaken. Thus, during the years in which the bulk of his organ music was written, Bach never had the regular use of an organ larger than two manuals and pedal, or with more than some twenty-five stops; though as a visitor he was well acquainted with many instruments, some of considerable size.

Registration must to some extent be a personal matter, involving the player's interpretation of the music's aesthetic and the particular nature of the instrument at his disposal. The developing of a good sense of appropriate tone colour will inevitably involve some study of Bach's organs and of the small amount of information available on contemporary registration.[22]

The suggestions which follow are for a medium-sized instrument, based on a 16′ Pedal Principal.

(a) Organo pleno

Principal chorus: 8′, 4′, 2⅔′, 2′, Mixture(s). (Sharp Mixtures higher than 1′ pitch at bottom C must be used with care, for they may disturb the listener's perception of line in complex contrapuntal music.) Secondary manual (preferably Positive): probably built on a Gedackt 8′, with Principal 4′ and Octave 2′. The Mixturework will be smaller and brighter than on the main chorus. Pedal: Principals 16′, 8′, 4′, Mixture, Trumpet 16′.[23]

(b) Some suggestions for trio combinations

My suggestions for flute registrations in Trios (given in Tables 4 and 5) are due to the desirability of pipework that forms a clear, attractive line, and that speaks promptly, with a good consonant. On finely voiced organs Principals might well be considered, particularly alone at 8′ pitch in slow movements. Note that the highest-sounding pitch of the left-hand registration should never be higher than that of the right hand.[24] The Tremulant in slow movements is optional (see end of Chapter 2). Note that the Tremulant can sometimes adversely affect the

---

[22] See 'Registration, general rules of' in Williams, *The European Organ (1450–1850)* (Batsford: London, 1966).

[23] Manual reeds are generally not used in the *organo pleno*, particularly when the music is highly contrapuntal, as they tend to cloud the clarity of line; this effect is especially noticeable with harmonic pipes or those using a heavier wind-pressure than the flue-work. It is better not to use a Pedal Mixture if its pitch is so high (and/or prominent) that it interferes with the listener's perception of the manual parts.

[24] There is considerable doubt as to whether or not Bach intended the use of 16′ pedal in his six sonatas (BWV 525–30), or indeed whether they were intended to be played on the organ, or on a double clavichord with pedal attachment. In the autograph, each sonata is headed 'à 2 Clav & Pedal'. However, in Bach's obituary of 1754, C. P. E. Bach and Agricola published an approximate list of Bach's works in which were mentioned 'Six trios for the organ, with obbligato pedal'. If they were intended for the organ, then we should consider the fact that the *Grund* or pedal foundation pitch was customarily 16′. However, as the sonatas are a unique translation of an instrumental idiom into organ terms, an 8′ pedal may perhaps uniquely be justified. Fortunately they sound well with either (despite the occasional inversion of l.h. and pedal parts); but if a 16′ pedal is used, it should be very light and prompt of speech. A full reasoning of this argument may be found on pp. 196 ff. of Walter Emery's *Notes on Bach's Organ Works: Six Sonatas for Two Manuals and Pedal* (Novello: London, 1957).

Table 4. Slow movements

Manual 1 (r.h.)	Manual II (l.h.)	Pedal
Flute 8′ (louder of the two)	Contrasted Flute 8′	Flute 8′
Flute 8′	Regal (or other quiet, characterful reed) 8′	Flute 8′
Flutes 8′, 4′	As above	Flute or fluty Principal 8′
Flute(s) 8′, (4′), Sesquialtera	Flutes 8′, 4′, or quiet reed	Flute(s) 8′, (4′), or fluty Principal 8′
Flute(s) 8′, (4′), $2\frac{2}{3}'$* (note the possibility of 4′ and $1\frac{1}{3}'$ played an octave lower)	Flute(s) 8′, (4′), or quiet reed	As above

    * NB: Not the $2\frac{2}{3}$ from the Principal chorus, but a fluty Nazard.

Table 5. Fast movements

Manual 1 (r.h.)	Manual II (l.h.)	Pedal
Flutes 8′, 2′ (or fluty 2′ Principal or Gemshorn)	Flutes 8′, 4′	Flutes 8′, 4′ or Principal 8′ (perhaps plus a *quiet* firm, quick-speaking 16′ flue-stop at the discretion of the player)
Flutes 8′, (4′), $1\frac{1}{3}'$	Flutes 8′, 2′	As above
Flutes 8′, 4′, 1′	Flutes 8′, 2′	As above, but the inclusion of a firm, though discreet, 4′ becomes more desirable
Flutes 8′, $2\frac{2}{3}'$, 1′	Flutes 8′, 2′ or 8′ 4′	As above
Flutes 8′, 2′, $1\frac{1}{3}'$	Flute 8′, Flute or Principal 4′	As above

speech or tuning of a short-length reed (e.g. the Regal family), and in such cases should not be used. In the five suggestions given for fast movements, it should be noted that, apart from the 8′ fundamental, the pitches of stops on the two manuals are not duplicated. This system lends clarity to interweaving musical lines, and while not always possible, is a principle that may usefully be borne in mind. The Tierce (1⅗′) is inappropriate in fast movements, as its introspective quality fights the music's essentially extrovert nature.

(c) Smaller-scale preludes and fugues

Lighter, more fluty registration may sometimes be appropriate, similar to that suggested for the right hand in fast trios; another possibility is the use of the Positive chorus rather than the Great. In each of these cases, the ear must determine an appropriate pedal balance, both in tonal and dynamic terms; where the pedal department is limited, the possibility of 'borrowing' stops for the pedal from an unused manual should also be remembered.

(d) Chorale preludes

1. The suggestions outlined in (a), (b), and (c) above each have a place, according to the nature of the music. In chorale trios, however, it is usually more appropriate to use a 16′ in the pedals, except where the pedal line is a cantus firmus at 8′ pitch (e.g. BWV 688) or at 4′ pitch (e.g. BWV 650).

2. In bold preludes which have a cantus firmus in the right hand (e.g. BWV 605, 657, 669) it would be appropriate to play the cantus firmus on Principals 8′, 4′, 2⅔′, 2′, Mixture (Trumpet 8′), with the left hand on the secondary chorus; or each hand on a suitably scaled-down (i.e. less harmonically developed) chorus. Bach did *not* possess a Tuba or other ultra-large-scale solo reed! However, a single chorus Trumpet 8′ for the cantus firmus against a suitable Principal chorus (probably without a Mixture) on the secondary manual would be a possibility; as might be the use of a really musical Cornet for right-hand solos. For a prelude such as 'Allein Gott' (BWV 663) in which the cantus firmus is in the left hand on a separate manual, one might even consider a 'tierce en taille' in the French manner (see Chapter 7); Bach knew well the cornet-sound from contemporary organs in Thuringia and Saxony, and such a registration would have been a most attractive possibility on—for example—the Rückpositiv division of the organ which he planned for Mühlhausen (see Appendix). Bach's own adventurousness and bold experimentation with organ registration is well documented; provided therefore that the student always bears in mind the nature of organs common to Bach's time and remembers always to use sounds

which underline the music's aesthetic, musical adventurousness is to be encouraged—though always in the service of the music.

3. In reflective preludes incorporating a varied solo line (e.g. BWV 622, 659, 662), one must be careful always to select registration in which the contrapuntal lines of the accompaniment may be clearly audible as an integral part of the music: a good rule is 'the simpler the better'.

For the working-out of the solo line itself, registrations appropriate to the music are of prime importance. Bach's chorale preludes (especially those of the *Orgel-Büchlein*) are works in which the words of the hymn are part of his musical concept; an awareness of the hymn's inner meaning and of its various theological aspects can be of great assistance in realizing a convincing interpretation; suitable registration is therefore the product of a careful study of the words and music in combination.

Possible registrations for solo lines (and their balanced accompaniment) may start with a perusal of those for slow movements given in (*b*) above; however, although a quiet reed may be suitable for the solo line, it would definitely be inappropriate for the accompaniment! Sometimes a quiet Principal 8′ can beautifully convey a solo line. At all times, the most persuasive and convincing interpretation is the aim, while the good taste of the player is the final arbiter.

7

The French Classical School

Music begins to atrophy when it departs too far from the dance . . .

(Ezra Pound)

THE period which spans roughly the reign of Louis XIV witnessed the first great flowering of the French organ and its music. The importance of Bach and the north German school at the turn of the seventeenth and eighteenth centuries has tended to overshadow that of the *grand siècle*[1] in terms of the development of the French organ and the music written for it. Modern musicology, particularly in America, has concentrated most of its efforts on the German culture of the period, and organ design has followed suit.[2] Had there been, since the 1930s, at least as much interest in the classical French organ school as in the German, the quality of musical interpretation upon the organ might well have been higher at the present time. The character of the French organ and its music demands a sensitivity to colour, line, and movement that can only be of immediate value to an emerging musician, and the modern student's curriculum should certainly include some study of this field.

The manner of performance in the *grand siècle*—the *goût français*—was well known in contemporary music circles abroad; its characteristic style is well documented, and idiomatic performance demands a working knowledge of its principles if the music is not to be misinterpreted.[3] The aspects of performance

[1] See Chapter 5, n. 2.

[2] However, one of the most comprehensive and scholarly accounts of French organ culture, up to and including this period, has been written by an American, Fenner Douglass: *The Language of the Classical French Organ* (Yale University Press: New Haven, 1969). His espousal of this great school has had a marked effect in generating contemporary interest in a culture which not only influenced the organ-builders of neighbouring countries, but also Bach himself.

[3] François Couperin was first among many French musicians who worried that posterity would be ignorant of their performance idiosyncrasies: 'the fact is we write a thing differently from the way in which we execute it; and it is this which causes foreigners to play our music less well than we do theirs. The Italians, on the contrary, write their music in the true time-values in which they have intended them to be played. For instance, we dot several consecutive quavers in diatonic succession, and yet we write them as equal; our custom has enslaved us, and we hold fast to it.' (*L'Art de toucher le Clavecin* (Paris, 1716); trans. Anna Linde, Breitkopf & Härtel: Wiesbaden, 1933), p. 23. Or perhaps the French—who were great encyclopaedists—were more particular than the sun-loving Italians; for it is inconceivable that any musical culture would perform music with no form of rhythmic flexibility, albeit not as detailed as the French style. As far as is known, Couperin never visited Italy.

discussed here relate particularly to the organ, though in many respects they are common to all music of the period.

Musical Style

Although it is not possible adequately to describe the *goût français* in a single word, to consider it as containing the technical and aesthetic attributes of singing might be useful. 'Singing' implies flexibility of line, rhythmic vitality, breathing, and emotional projection; all these characteristics are presented in the *goût français*. They are also, of course, considerations in the performance of those singing lines which form the contrapuntal basis of other schools, including Bach. But as the French characteristics are technically idiosyncratic, their study is as important as would be, for instance, the learning of ornamentation.

(a) *The importance of lightness and space*

Musical performance in this period tends to balance a feeling for lightness and the dance with the necessity for continuity of line: too much emphasis on light-ness can detract from forward movement, while an exclusive preoccupation with line can diminish the airy grace inherent in rhythmic groups. Although impor-tant in other schools of composition, this balance is nowhere more stylistically critical than in that of the *grand siècle*. Lightness is evidenced by such considera-tions as the ends of phrases—in which their frequently 'throw-away' nature makes clear the importance of trochaic metre,[4]

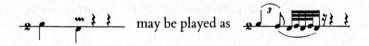

while the composite notes of a musical line must be viewed in association with the space (or silence) that often lies between them, not in the technical sense of *silences d'articulation*, but as an expressive device yielding space, breadth, or vivacity according to the nature of the music. This technique of 'aspiration' is specifically marked in harpsichord music of the period. Couperin's sign for it is ⦙ , and in *L'Art de toucher le clavecin* (Paris, 1716) he exhorts the player to be sensitive to its context: 'the note over which [the sign] is placed must be detached less abruptly in passages which are tender and slow than in those which are light

---

[4] e.g. François Couperin, 'Récit de Chromhorne' from *Messe pour les Paroisses*, bar 32; consider also bars 9 and 16.

and quick.'[5] All music must breathe if it is to live, and although the sign for aspiration is not used in organ music, the principle is no less important; for organ tones lack even the natural inflexion of harpsichord sounds. Indeed, as we saw in Chapter 4, the musical application of 'space' to organ music can be one of the most vitalizing expressive techniques available to the organist; it is certainly one of the most necessary.

In Ex. 7.1(*a*), an extract from the 'Benedictus' in François Couperin's *Messe pour les Paroisses*,[6] a sense of parlando (played as shown in Ex. 7.1(*b*) can lend piquancy to the repeated notes. In quick music, aspiration adds zest to rhythmic

Ex. 7.1

momentum: fingertip lightness in the 'Duo sur les Tierces' (Ex. 7.2), as implied by my suggested phrasing, will make the lines sparkle; while at a subsidiary cadence in the same piece (Ex. 7.3), the shift of accent from two in each bar to three (hemiola) can be given extra spice if articulated with plenty of space between the dotted quaver and semiquaver.

Similarly, long sustained notes may be shortened. The right-hand chords in the 'Dialogue sur les Trompettes' (Ex. 7.4), if played in a resonant room exactly as

Ex. 7.2

Ex. 7.3

---

[5] *L'Art de toucher le clavecin*, p. 15.
[6] Ex. 7.2–4 are also taken from this work.

Ex. 7.4

written, would almost inevitably be perceived as overlapping to a greater or lesser extent; separating them a little, as shown, not only clarifies the music but also gives it more character. A working knowledge of the fingering system in use when this music was written can only be of the greatest assistance to the player in achieving a naturally graceful, airy style; it enables him to be sympathetic to the possibility of natural note groupings, and it encourages him to be more aware of the function of 'space' in achieving idiomatic grace and excitement (see Chapter 5).

(b) Notes inégales

The French manner, in an appropriate musical context, often gives a more lilting aspect to pairs of adjacent notes than would be the case if they were played literally. Such *inégalité* forms the principal rhythmic characteristic of the period, and was based on the natural expression of the singer, who stressed the main accent in rhythmic structures. As the keyboard player's equivalent of stress included the possibility of lengthening the accented note, so the custom of lengthening one note at the expense of the next grew and was gradually codified.

Although there must always be an element of uncertainty in attempting to recreate the idiomatic style of this period (let alone that of individual composers), enough is known from several contemporary treatises to construct a basic system upon which the student can build for himself a more detailed understanding of the music and its performance. Three types of *inégalité* were used in the *grand siècle* as follows.

1. *Lourer* (grouping). This is the most commonly encountered form in which ♫ becomes approximately ♩ ♪ in melodies where the notes follow one another by step. In practice, the degree of inequality can vary from a single shortening of the second note ████ , through ████ , to trip-

lets ♩♪♩♪ , to ♪.♩♪.♩ or even more, depending on the aesthetic demands of the music. In its slightest form, it would assume the character of an agogic accent. In fact, only the *goût* of the player can decide whether the degree of inequality is to be greater or lesser, though as a general guide it will be more subtle in tender music, and more pronounced where the movement is lively. A small change of degree can make a big difference to the music's expressiveness, and the degree of inequality can vary within the same piece of music; the player must therefore involve his ear and his heart at least as much as his fingers.

The time-value of the note-pairs which will be subject to inequality in a particular piece is determined by the time signature, as shown in Table 6. Of the groups illustrated there, organists are principally concerned with B and C, C being the most common.

Table 6. Note-pairs subject to *inégalité*

	Time Signature	Note-pairs subject to inequality
A	3/1	♩ ♩
B	3/2	♩ ♩ and ♫
C	2, 3, 3/4, 6/4, 9/4, 12/4, ¢ (when 2-in-a-bar), occasionally C and 2/4*	♫
D	4, 2/4, 4/4, 3/8, 4/8, 6/8, 9/8, 12/8, C, ¢ (when 4-in-a-bar)	♬
E	3/16, 4/16, 6/16, etc.	♬

* The movement of the piece is the deciding factor; if four square, quaver inequality is not appropriate.

There are several important exceptions: pairs of notes are *not* played *inégales* in the following circumstances:

   (i) when they move by interval, and their movement is essentially harmonic (e.g. arpeggios);
  (ii) when they are repetitions of the same note;
 (iii) when they are syncopated;
 (iv) when they are mixed with many rests of the same value;
  (v) in passages moving very quickly;
 (vi) in vigorous music which is essentially four square;

(vii) where dots or dashes are placed above the notes;

(viii) when pairs of notes are slurred ♫ or ♫ , or several pairs are slurred together;

(ix) when the music is marked otherwise (*notes égales*, *martelées*, *détachées*, *mouvement decidé ou marqué*).

Rests are subject to the same degree of *inégalité* used in the notes around them.

2. *Piquer* (pricking) or *pointer* (dotting). In music in which the pairs of notes ♫ are played *lourer* ♩ ♪, dotted groups ♪. ♪ are similarly stretched, and may be played ♪.. ♪ ; the short note should be played very lightly, as though belonging to the following beat.

3. *Couler* (flowing). Pairs of notes moving by step and slurred ♪ ♩ or ♩ ♪ should be played ♫.

Once *inégalité* is decided upon for a certain piece, it should be used throughout (or for a clearly defined section of it), and not confined to *ad hoc* phrases; and just as the degree of *inégalité* can vary in the course of a piece, so also it may be sharpened at cadences, and may even occur at cadences of pieces in which *inégalité* has not been employed.

The music of the *grand siècle* requires not just the application of rules, but also a quality of interpretation which springs from an understanding of melody and rhythm, and from the gradual development of the free and sympathetic style that is the essence of the player's *bon goût*. The points made in these few pages form the briefest outline of the basic requirements for interpretation. Having absorbed them, the student must then read as widely as possible, and, most important of all, play the music of the period, preferably on an organ with highly responsive mechanical action. The best form of education in this, as in any other period, is constant immersion in the music.

The Organ, and Registration upon it

Perhaps it was the Frenchman's passionate love of singing that affected the evolution of the organ more than that of any other instrument of the seventeenth and eighteenth centuries. Certain tonal features introduced by Netherlands builders a century earlier were gradually developed into colours which, by their richness, came close to representing the more obvious characteristics of colour in the human voice. Singing also played a part in the organ's design, as exemplified by the development of the pedals into a division the principal purpose of which was to provide (at 8´ pitch) the fluty bass line of a trio, or a brassy cantus firmus. Except occasionally in Southern France, the *Pédale* had no 16´ stops of its own; its *raison d'être* was purely lyrical.[7]

Composers of organ music from 1660 onwards became gradually more specific as to the tone colours to be used, and the title or subtitle of a work often forms a description of the required registration, e.g. *Tierce en taille*, *Plein jeu*, *Trio à 2 dessus de chromhorne et la basse de tierce*, etc. Additionally, there is often an aesthetic association between the indicated tone colours and the mood of the music: *Tierce en taille* is invariably plangent and haunting, but a *Duo sur les tierces* is gay and lively; a piece for the *Voix humaine* is usually piquantly delicate; *Basse de trompette* is at once vigorous and majestic—and so on.

Originally *jeu* meant 'one stop', but the term gradually broadened to mean 'a collection of stops'; indeed, for some while prior to the 1630s, the two meanings were used indiscriminately. But by the time of the *grand siècle*, *jeu* was used to denote a generic sound arising from the juxtaposition of several stops.

The *plein jeu* was the counterpart of today's Principal chorus—the foundation of organ tone. It consisted of Bourdon 16´ and 8´, Montre 8´, Prestant 4´, Doublette 2´, Fourniture, and Cymbale. The combination was used for preludes, which were largely homophonic and of a stately demeanour. If the prelude was constructed around a plainsong cantus firmus, this would be played on the pedals, using the brilliant Trompette 8´, either coupled to the *Grand orgue* or not, according to the demands of the music.[8] *Grand plein jeu* means the *plein jeu* of the *Grand orgue* coupled with a similar tonal make-up on the *Postif*. The combination must not be confused with the *Grands jeux*. André Raison writes that 'a *Grand plein jeu* is played very slowly. The chords should be quite legato one to the other, taking pains not to raise one finger until the other has passed down,[9] and the last measure should be much prolonged. The *Petit plein jeu* is played lightly and fluently.'[10] The latter would be played on the *Positif*. Ornamentation in music written for the *Grand plein jeu* is kept to a minimum.

The other classic chorus of the French organ, and unique to it, is the *Grands jeux*. Basically, it consists of Trompettes and Cornets. Contemporary musicians

---

[7] However, the *Grand Orgue* usually contained a 16´ Bourdon, and very occasionally a 16´ Montre *en façade* as well.

[8] A Great to Pedal coupler (*Tirasse G.O.*) is sometimes referred to in contemporary writings—e.g. the preface to Jacques Boyvin's *Premier Livre d'Orgue* (1689)—but is thought to have been by no means commonly provided at this time. Remember that French pedal-keys were rather short, often awkward, and convenient only for a relatively slow-moving line.

[9] Raison's intention is to preserve a full flowing harmony; but if his instructions were to be followed too literally, the listener in a resonant building might be assailed by overlapping vowel sounds (see comments on touch in Chapter 4).

[10] André Raison, *Livre d'orgue* (1688); trans. Douglass, ibid., p. 185.

of the period differ over the question of including the 8′ Montre (or Principal). Otherwise, the registration for the *Grands jeux* is of the following order: Bourdon 8′, Prestant 4′, Doublette 2′, Nazard 2⅔′, Tierce 1⅗′, Cornet, Trompette 8′, and perhaps Clairon 4′. Registration on the *Positif* is similar, with the Chromhorne 8′ substituted for the Trompette. The essence of this tonal combination is that it forms a rich, reedy, *homogeneous* sound in which no specific colour or pitch obtrudes; it represents resplendent architecture in sound—a building which transcends its individual features. Its homogeneous nature thus enables the movement of contrapuntal lines to be clearly distinguished, and *Grands jeux* is used in *dialogues* and in large-scale compositions such as *offertoires*, in which dialogue between alternating manuals frequently plays a part. *Fugues graves*, however, are generally not played on the full *grands jeux* but on a combination of Flute 8′, Prestant 4′, Trompette 8′, and possibly the Clairon as well; on a small organ on the Petit Bourdon and Cromorne 8′. The *fugue gaye* is played on something more brilliant—Chaumont suggests 'the Pettite Tierce, Bourdon, Montre, Nazard, etc.'.[11]

For other colour combinations there are innumerable possibilities. Although the number of combinations in frequent use is comparatively small, different composers vary in the detail of their recommendations; but this is hardly surprising, as each will have been influenced by the organ commonly at his disposal, as well as by regional variations in organ design and by the popular taste of his own time and neighbourhood. The reader is therefore urged to read the most commonly available prefaces by Nivers (1665), LeBègue (1676), Raison (1688), Gaspard Corrette (1703), and others, all of which and more are translated in Fenner Douglass's book. Registration is always an artistic challenge, and the player would do well to bear in mind a dictum of Jacques Boyvin, that 'one of the most beautiful ornaments of the organ comes from knowing how to combine stops'.[12]

As a preliminary guide, there follows a brief list of the colours most commonly called for.

Tierce en taille. Accompaniment: Bourdon 8′, Prestant[13] or Flute 4′; or perhaps Bourdons 16′ and 8′. Pedal, Flute 8′, or perhaps coupled to the *Grand Orgue* instead. Solo (usually on the *Positif*): Bourdon 8′, Prestant (or Flute) 4′, Nazard

---

[11] Lambert Chaumont, *Livre d'orgue* (1695); trans. Douglass, ibid., p. 193.

[12] Jacques Boyvin, *Premier Livre d'orgue* (1689); trans. Douglass, ibid., p. 186.

[13] Note that this was a sweet, clear, open metal stop often placed *en façade*; it is not to be confused with the Principal 4′ of the north German schools, which often produced a much sharper, dominating sound. On modern organs it is infinitely preferable to select a 4′ Flute than an unsuitably forthright Principal.

$2\frac{2}{3}'$, Doublette (a fluty principal) $2'$, Tierce $1\frac{3}{5}'$, Larigot $1\frac{1}{3}'$. This combination should be rich and homogeneous—like the voice of a solo tenor.

Chromhorne en taille. Accompaniment: as above. Solo: Chromhorne $8'$, Bourdon $8'$, Prestant (or Flute) $4'$, and perhaps the Nazard $2\frac{2}{3}'$.

Dessus, or *Récit de chromhorne.* This would probably use neither the $4'$ nor the $2\frac{2}{3}'$. If the Chromhorne is attractive, it may even be used on its own. The accompaniment would be Bourdon $8'$ alone, or with the addition of a Flute $4'$ if the tone of the $8'$ proved indeterminate or unclear.

Récit de Nazard. In common with all *Récits* (except the Chromhorne), the accompaniment is Bourdon $8'$, Prestant $4'$ (or, if too strong, Flute $4'$). Pedal, Flute $8'$. The solo in this case is Bourdon $8'$ (Flute $4'$ at the player's discretion), Nazard $2\frac{2}{3}'$, occasionally Larigot $1\frac{1}{3}'$ (but remember the sound must be sweet).

Récit de Tierce. As *Récit de Nazard* above, with the addition in the solo line of the Tierce and perhaps the Doublette as well.

Récit de Cornet. Accompaniment as above, the solo being played on a *Cornet separé*, i.e. drawn on one stop; this contrasts with the *Jeu de tierces*, which consists basically of the same composite ranks drawn on individual stops. According to Raison, 'the Cornet is played with celerity, animation and fluidity; and the chief cadences should be lengthened, especially the last.'[14]

Voix humaine. Any piece involving the Voix humaine assumes the addition of the Bourdon $8'$, and often Flute $4'$ as well, plus most commonly the *Tremblant doux*. Pieces for *Voix humaine* are almost always played tenderly.

Duo. This is commonly played on two Tierces: in the right hand (usually the *Positif*) Bourdon $8'$, Prestant $4'$, Nazard, and Tierce; in the left hand, the same plus the Quarte de Nazard (a $2'$ Flute) or failing that the Doublette $2'$, and—if there is one—perhaps a Gros Nazard $5\frac{1}{3}'$, Tierce $3\frac{1}{5}'$, and a $16'$ Bourdon. When written in quavers it is invariably played rapidly and pointedly. On individual organs homogeneity must be the guide as to which stops are used.

Trio. The trio often uses the Chromhorne alone in the right hand, with the Bourdon $8'$, Prestant $4'$, Nazard, Quarte de Nazard, and Tierce in the left hand. Raison (1688) suggests an unusually ear-catching combination for a gentle trio of his own—right hand: Bourdon, Flute [$8'$ or $4'$?], and Nazard, with *Tremblant doux*; l.h.: Voix humaine, Bourdon $8'$, Flute [$8'$ or $4'$?—most probably $4'$].

Basse de Trompette (ou Chromhorne). The left hand is given to the Trompette $8'$ plus Bourdon $8'$ and Prestant $4'$, and the right hand (on another manual) to Bourdon $8'$ and a suitable $4'$.

---

[14] Raison, *Livre d'orgue* (1688); trans. Douglass, ibid., p. 184.

Ornamentation

A detailed study of ornamentation in the *grand siècle* is beyond the scope of this book, and the reader is urged to undertake further study from the literature noted in the Reading List. However, a brief survey of ornamentation may be useful, as the intelligent and sensitive interpretation of signs is perhaps more essential to music of this period than to that of any other in the organ repertory.

It is worth repeating that the fingers should be curled, with the tips remaining close to the keys and not lifted high away from them, so that minimum physical movement is required to achieve an even, crisp legato. The arm and hand must always be completely relaxed, with energy concentrated in the fingers alone.

(a) Trills (*tremblements*)

These begin on the upper auxiliary and start on the beat unless slurred to the previous note; their beginning and end must be pointed (to a greater or lesser degree, depending on the liveliness or otherwise of the music) so that the ornament is played as an entity. Couperin tells us that 'Shakes of any considerable duration consist of three component parts, which in the execution appear to be but one and the same thing: 1, L'Appuy (sustaining, dwelling) to be made on the note above the principal note; 2, Les batemens (the repercussions); 3, Le point d'arest (the stop).

With regard to other sorts of shakes, they are arbitrary. There are some which have the "dwelling" on the upper auxiliary note; others so short that they have neither the "dwelling" nor the final "stop" (point-d'arest). One can even play shakes "aspirés" (cut short, ending with an abrupt rest.)[15]

Unless very short, *tremblements* should begin more slowly than they finish. In brief, we may distinguish three representative types:

tremblement appuyé

---

[15] *L'Art de toucher le clavecin*, p. 18.

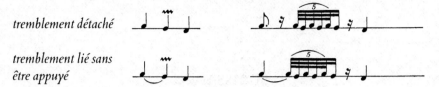

tremblement détaché

tremblement lié sans être appuyé

(b) Appoggiaturas (ports de voix)

The *port de voix* is essentially a melodic decoration which came to have increasing harmonic significance. It can appear as a hook[16]  or as a small note either ascending or descending, and is played on the beat, though in some contexts it may be shorter or longer than half the value of the main note. A *port de voix* anticipates the beat, however, when slurred to the previous note, and when joining the notes of descending thirds (like the German *Nachschlag*), in which form it assumes a particularly graceful air.[17]

(c) Mordent (pincé)

These are played on the beat in the manner followed by all other schools of the period. They may be either short (*simple*) or longer (*doublé*)

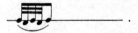

(d) Port de voix avec pincé

A combination of appoggiatura and mordent.

(e) The turn (cadence)

This usually 'turns around' the note over which the sign appears.

[16] Not to be confused with the *Coulé* played.

[17] The *port de voix* can also be indicated by a cross (+). In the table of ornaments given by Boyvin, ibid., he illustrates crosses between descending thirds as appoggiaturas sounding on the beat.

8

Renaissance

Change is not made without inconvenience, even from worse to better.

(Richard Hooker, sixteenth century)

The Instrument

THE early twentieth-century demise of the organ as a medium for musical expression (temporary though it proved to be) was neatly, poetically, and devastatingly summarized by Arnold Dolmetsch in 1916, when the instrument's artistic fortunes were at their lowest ebb.

The organ remained faithful to the old ideals longer than other instruments. The makers of 1815 worked much on the same principles as those of 1615. In most houses there was a little organ, soft and sweet, easy to play, ready to warble like a bird, or with two stops to make you feel the ecstasies of God's worship. The church organs in addition had that power based on sweetness which constitutes majesty. The change came on, and for the sake of louder tone, pressure of wind was doubled and trebled. The same pressure acting on the valves which let the wind into the pipes made them too heavy for the fingers to move through the keys. A machine was then invented which did the work at second hand. Instead of shutting your own door, if you call a servant to do so, the door may get shut, but not so quickly. So the music of the organ dragged on after the player's fingers as best it could. Personal touch, which did so much for phrasing and expression, was destroyed.[1]

Even organists' loyalties at this time showed symptoms of strain and confusion. One of the best musicians and teachers of the period bravely wrote that 'clarity, rhythmical control and intelligent phrasing are the first essentials of good organ playing. . . . and must always take precedence over such matters as power, colour and registration in general';[2] later in the same article, however, one detects a whiff of frustration as the writer notes that 'the lack of "bite" in the speech of the organ tends to dull the player's sense of time and rhythm. Lacking the stimulus of

---

[1] *The Interpretation of Music*, p. 436.
[2] G. D. Cunningham, 'Organ playing', *Grove's Dictionary of Music and Musicians* (5th edition), Vol. 6, p. 344.

the [piano's] hammer-blow, the organist must himself the more vividly feel the exact "time-spot" of every note.' Such an ineffectual attack, so keenly regretted, was the result of servo-action, high-pressure wind, and an often drastic modification of pipe-mouths so as to suppress (or at least firmly to control) any transient 'chiff' as the pipes spoke.

The best players knew—in theory, at any rate—that in terms of musical expressiveness the organs of the early years of the twentieth century fell far short of the possibilities offered by any other instrument. Small wonder, then, that so many frustrated musicians forsook the organ for other fields; though a few stayed to keep artistic imagination alive until eventually this 'pernicious tendency which had been creeping into organ design since the early days of Cavaillé-Coll'[3] exhausted itself and renaissance began.

The Player

However, a revolution in organ design—hesitant and painful though it may be— is easier to achieve than is a balanced musical outlook amongst players. A phenomenon of the second half of the twentieth century is the existence, side by side, of students with widely differing assumptions about the organ's musical role. They were born in an age of confusion when advocacy, of either the 'old' style or the 'new', led often to partisanship and mutual intolerance; as a result, it is no more uncommon today for a student to regard music written before 1870 as old-fashioned than it is for his contemporary (with a different teacher) to view anything written after 1750 as decadent; and the same might well apply to their views on organs. Of the two extremes, however, it is arguable that the latter might more successfully be weaned to more catholic fare. The music of the great Romantic composers follows upon the historical precepts of their forebears; the expressive nuances of Franck's best music on the great symphonic instruments of Cavaillé-Coll are more intelligently handled by the player who has known the *grands jeux* of Couperin and the rhythmic flexibility of the *grand siècle*; while the textural complexities of Reger's great chorale fantasies are more easily unravelled and presented in intelligible dialogue by the student well versed in projecting the singing musical lines of J. S. Bach. Style and idiom apart, the basic principles of aural projection (touch, articulation, expressive devices) learnt in the process of realizing seventeenth- and eighteenth-century music are in fact largely the

---

[3] W. L. Sumner, *The Organ: Its Evolution, Principles of Construction and Use* (MacDonald: London, 1952), pp. 228–9: the author is describing the excesses of the Hope-Jones 'one-man orchestra', which represents the nadir of the classical organ.

common performance techniques of all tonal organ music; and they are essential to the intelligent exploration of new idioms for the instrument's future. Of course, significant idiomatic differences emerge from age to age, and vary from one country to another. These may well affect the degree of articulátion; they will certainly involve different concepts of line and phrasing, together with a modified approach to expressive matters; while the music's country of origin will suggest tone colours appropriate to the organs for which the composer was writing. None of these modifications, however, affects the basic physical principles of aural communication between the performer and his audience. The music must always be communicated as intelligibly, and hence with as much *Affekt*, as an actor, for example, would declaim Shakespeare or Bernard Shaw. Individual realizations of each author may well differ widely, while interpretations of Shakespeare will all differ idiomatically from those of Shaw; but, regardless of the author's style or period, only the failed actor will be unintelligible, or will string together his syllables in a manner devoid of accent or inflexion.

The Composer

In considering style and idiom after the mid-eighteenth century, no organ music of serious consequence is known for about ninety years: the best of what there is includes some lightweight concertos and 'clock' pieces from Haydn, while Mozart wrote sixteen church sonatas for organ and other instruments. Mozart also wrote two fantasias for mechanical 'flute clocks', and these have been preserved in innumerable subsequent transcriptions for organ. The organ did not suit the style of the period, while the musical manners of the time did not suit the organ. Even by 1750 the true Baroque style of performance, with its gentle taste and elegant neatness, was fast giving way to extravagance; subtle expressive devices were lost in over-articulation, excessive ornamentation, and an air of breathless drama; counterpoint was rather a dull exercise (though C. P. E. Bach's father was a legend long after his death); and organs were losing their disciplined tonal structure. In the excitement of a new era, the organ was left on the sidelines of music.

In 1835, at the age of twenty-six Mendelssohn became conductor of the Gewandhaus concerts in Leipzig—a city of fine organs, including many by Silbermann. In 1837, on the new organ of Birmingham Town Hall, he played the Prelude and Fugue which frame the third part of Bach's *Clavier-Übung* (and put the two pieces together probably for the first time); and in this same year he completed three preludes and fugues which he dedicated to his great friend and admirer Thomas Attwood, organist of St Paul's Cathedral in London. Seven years later came six sonatas, and with this slim *œuvre*, the organ's repertory was revitalized; unequal though the music may be, it draws on the contrapuntal technique of Bach, owes something to Classical form, yet is full of the new Romanticism. One has only to glance at the A major Sonata to see clearly these three elements boldly combined in an eminently stylistic whole. The organ works of Mendelssohn thus form a distinct 'period' of their own, and much may be gained from their study by the student searching for an interpretational link between the Baroque and the Romantic. Mendelssohn, like Bach a century earlier, was known for an imaginative use of colour in his organ performances: this was the imagination of the musician of broad interests, whose ear has experienced a wider spectrum than can be envisaged from the insular confines of an organ-loft. Yet from our knowledge of Mendelssohn's precise—even fussy— sense of style (abhorring excessive rubato, for example), it seems likely that his registrations were more sympathetic with the terraced dynamics of the Baroque, and 'the power based on sweetness' of Silbermann, than prophetic of the symphonic organ sounds of half a century later. For the late twentieth-century organist, peering back at Mendelssohn through an impressionistic haze of pre- renaissance Large Open Diapasons and English Full Swells, the temptation to play his slow movements with one foot on the swell pedal can finally be overcome only by some experience of playing the sonatas, ideally, on a fine eighteenth-century organ—or even on a modern classical instrument if that is not possible.

The first great Romantic composer for the organ was César Franck, who was twenty-four when Mendelssohn died in 1847. His best music came relatively late in his life, and the whole corpus of his organ music is quite small: *Six pièces* (1862), *Trois pièces* (1878), and *Trois chorals* (1890), plus two collections of very uneven small pieces intended mainly for the harmonium. Franck's style is highly personal and easily recognizable through its harmonic idiom and methods of construction. The essentially contemplative, singing quality of his best music often emerges paradoxically from segmental writing reminiscent of two hundred years earlier; in his *Fantaisie* in A may be seen examples both of the characteristic segmented phrase of which the music's form is an enlarged image (Ex. 8.1) and of the sort of line whose forward sweep is conceived in the broadest terms (Ex. 8.2). The interpretation of Franck's music might therefore more easily be envisaged by the student who has also studied the problems of continuity in toccatas (or *preludes*) by Frescobaldi or Bruhns or Buxtehude: such music encourages an appreciation of structure and form, and of the expressive aesthetic that binds segments into a cohesive entity.

A constant characteristic of French organ schools from the seventeenth century

Ex. 8.1

Ex. 8.2

to the present day is their often rigorous insistence on registrational colour as an essential ingredient of the music's conception; for 'the right sound' in much French organ music is akin to orchestration, in the sense that tone colour and musical aesthetic are inextricably intertwined.

The two or three decades from 1930 were years of great revelation and innovation in France, where the historic tradition of the organist-composer was carried forward by such men as Marcel Dupré, Jehan Alain, and Olivier Messiaen. Each, while retaining the precepts of the past, turned a new page in the history of the organ's potential, though the early death of Alain at the age of twenty-nine left Messiaen to become the most profound influence of the twentieth century on French organ composition. Messiaen's combination of unique harmonic and rhythmic concepts, and carefully 'orchestrated' colour has produced one of the most easily identifiable—and often imitated—styles in the history of music. No modern student's education is complete without the study of a representative selection of his *œuvre*; and such a study should include the challenge of at least one very slow piece in which the player's ability to sustain a convincing continuity of line will be severely tested (see Reading List, pp. 148–9).

Outside France, no organ tradition developed comparable with that of the French symphonic school represented by Franck, Widor, Vierne, and Tournemire; and at no time did tone colour in the widest sense ever play an integral part in the concept of organ music outside France. Germany saw no great organ composer between Mendelssohn and Reger (1873–1916) except in occasional and useful forays by such men as Schumann, Liszt, and Brahms; though from the evidence of one major programmatic work of genius, Julius Reubke (1834–58) might well have proved to be such a figure, had he lived to a riper age.

Today's revolution in the art of the organ seems, in the 1980s, to be concerned comparatively little with organ composition. What there is can be divided into (1) music which reflects the forms and styles of the past in tonal or atonal language of the present, and (2) music which seeks to break new ground in terms of the instrument's technical potential. The latter may perhaps be divided in turn into (*a*) compositions which utilize the organ's tonal and dynamic possibilities in descriptive music or music in which *Affekt* plays an important part, and (*b*) music which seeks to further the organ's eminent suitability for line and counterpoint. A combination of these two approaches would seem to present an ideal challenge to composers. However, a comprehensive knowledge of the organ's historical nature, its repertory, and, above all, its interpretative techniques is not generally to be found in modern composers, who seldom seem able to recognize and play upon more than the instrument's most superficial characteristics of sustained tone, colour, and sheer noise.

If organ music is to be convincing, *movement* is essential, and obfuscation must actively be avoided: both of these requirements are answered in good contrapuntal writing. To this end, every young composer's study repertoire should include the three organ sonatas (1937-40) of Paul Hindemith. These neglected works reflect a carefully researched knowledge of the instrument, an awareness of the organ's supreme suitability for expressive counterpoint, and a sympathy with organ techniques which mark them as a breakthrough in twentieth-century composition. They respect the lessons of history, while being eminently products of their own time; and like all worthwhile music, they challenge the performer's musical expressiveness rather than simply testing his digital capabilities. As with all that is best in the organ's repertory, a sense of the beauty of line is the first essential in their interpretation. They also demonstrate the truth that, as an interpretative instrument, the organ responds best to music containing as few notes as possible, in the sense that the best art employs an economy of means in which superfluous strokes—of the pen or the brush—are ruthlessly suppressed. 'Big is best' only when largeness is a necessary concomitant of the art's expressive nature; and 'small is beautiful' when it is the result of disciplined thought, and not simply a less glorious version of 'big'.

Economy of means and disciplined thought are twin essentials in the art of improvisation. This thrilling skill, so invigorating to true composition, is less popular amongst organists now than at any time over the past fifty years, despite many efforts to encourage it in young musicians through teaching and competitions. Its decline may well be connected with the dearth of good, new composition: composers are perhaps less likely to provide new music for an instrument if its own players are reluctant (or unable) to do so; or if, when they do, they tend chiefly to exploit its more superficial aspects; tonal effect and sheer noise, especially if devoid of musical reasoning, can be repellent to music lovers. As with composed music, the most satisfying improvisation springs from a seed of inspiration developed and nurtured by the ministrations of hands which have known the sweat and labour of practising harmony, counterpoint, and form.

Such essential disciplines, however, take time to learn and to absorb into the subconscious, and time nowadays seems to be at a premium. Many students want to make an impression upon the public as soon as they have learnt the bare notes of a major repertory work: interpretation is sometimes grudging, even perfunctory, and the resulting exploitation of the organ's aural potential too often results in one more disservice to the art of making music on the organ. Perhaps it is only an even higher standard of critical appreciation amongst listeners that will eventually encourage in young players a sharper awareness of the musical potential of their instrument, of the musical styles and forms which suit it best, and of the prime necessity for discipline in their approach to playing. In such a climate, it is probable that improvisation once again will flourish, with composition as its handmaiden.

Integrity and the Student's Objectives

The most appropriate approach to great music of a certain style and period is generally found to occur most naturally on instruments of the same period and country of origin as the music's composer. The player's touch unconsciously responds to such specifics as the instrument's action and the size of the keys, while his interpretative response to the music is intensified by the sound of the instrument and even by the ergonomic layout of the console. The compact nature of a seventeenth- or eighteenth-century console (smaller manual and pedal keys, placed closer to the player, and fewer of them) feels distinctively suited to the nature of the music of the period; on good instruments articulation becomes less contrived, and tempo more instinctively appropriate to the music. By comparison, the console of a late nineteenth-century instrument is broader .and more spacious; it is altogether better suited to the nature of the music of its own time, from the keys, to the distance between the manuals, to the size and disposition of the pedals, to the sound of pipes on higher-pressure wind. On early twentieth-century organs, the lack of oneness between the player and instrument engendered by servo-actions and by an even more roomy console environment was well suited to the contemporary repertory, which all too often relied heavily upon aural effect to underpin music of stylized prosiness. Small wonder, then, that in such a cultural environment contrapuntal interpretation was a stranger. Many such instruments still exist, either unsullied by subsequent developments, or (more likely) incorporating some superficial traits of renaissance thought. Better by far that they be left as honest instruments of their time, that the best be faithfully restored, and the worst recognized for their failings and completely replaced. For the updating of an instrument tends only to emphasize its shortcomings; the best student is confused by the absence of a homogeneous style and by the lack of that simple integrity which he has most likely already experienced with the piano.

If there are two paramount objects in an organ student's education, the first is the acquisition of a sense of integrity in the combining of music, instrument, and interpretation: not to encourage narrowness of thought or purism of outlook in the musician, but in order to create a yardstick of excellence. The situation where the instrument and the music are ideally matched is of course extremely rare. Comparatively few historic instruments exist, though modern organs in different classic styles (for example, French Romantic as well as regional Baroque) are beginning to appear from specialist builders. The majority of large organs will continue for some time to be eclectic instruments, built in concert halls to try to provide at least approximately suitable tone colour for an impossibly wide compositional spectrum, or in churches to accompany the liturgy and only occasionally to be used in recital. Unless, therefore, an organist is to be content with the restrictions implied by making music only on historically appropriate instruments—a measure practicable only in a country possessing many historic organs—he would be wise to develop the ability to adopt a pragmatic approach to tone colour and performance techniques when necessary. To this end, he should have experienced the feel of period instruments, should have their individualistic sound in his mind, and must be aware of the tone colours belonging to specific areas of organ music; without such experience and learning, he has no yardstick when seeking suitable colour and attempting an appropriate performing style on a modern eclectic instrument.

Recordings made on period instruments can provide a substitute for personally experiencing the instruments in their native environment, but only to a very limited extent; for no recording can adequately convey such subtleties as the totality of the organ in its building, or the aural perspective of the *Rückpositiv* against the *Hauptwerk*, let alone that vital feel of the instrument under the player's hands. Nevertheless, recording can be useful in an initial exploration of tone colour, enabling the student to distinguish such basics as the *grands jeux* from the *plein jeu*, or *organo pleno* on a Silbermann from a plenum with and without reeds on a Cavaillé-Coll, and in discovering the many interpretative subtleties that may distinguish one performance from another.

The second paramount necessity for an organ student is to relate his music-making to that of musicians in other instrumental fields. Any performer who tries to live in an environment insulated from other music-making will atrophy; his playing will become personalized and subjective, and he may well develop an antagonism towards his listeners, whom he will probably dismiss as ignorant or unsympathetic. This danger is particularly acute for an organist, whose console is often physically remote from his audience, and whose instrument has the capability of dominating the listener rather than wooing him. Such problems are marvellously countered by a healthy curiosity towards other musical genres, especially those involving wind instruments (including the voice), and forms in which musical line is especially important, such as the string quartet. With the experience of such kindred music, the organist is less likely to accept as normal such anti-musical fashions as unremitting *détaché* (or legato), which he would be amongst the first to question in other genres.

The organ renaissance today needs living, breathing, sensitive players. Fifty years ago, when public appreciation of the symphony orchestra was highly sophisticated, the organ was regarded as a liturgical Muzak machine. The step from such an attitude to one of simple respect—let alone affection—requires patience, tuition, musical sensitivity, and a strong commitment to real music-making. At the time of writing, the old mould has been broken, and a new one is being forged. Music which until quite recently has been the sole province of organists and 'organ buffs' is being gradually assimilated into the broad spectrum of musical performance as a whole. The omens are good, given musical vision.

APPENDIX I: THE WORKING OF THE ORGAN'S KEYBOARD ACTION:
A classic illustration of the need for excellence.

The principal features of organ construction have changed little since the Benedictine monk François Bédos de Celles (generally known as Dom Bédos) published *L'Art du Facteur d'Orgues* (Paris, 1766–78). Good organ-building still depends on enough continuous wind fed to the windchests through trunks of an appropriate cross-section, and on the pallets being opened and closed via a key-action which accurately represents the player's minutest articulative intentions.

Given these principles, the gulf between a poor organ and a good one is bridged by garnered knowledge and relentless endeavour; by meticulous design and draughtsmanship; by an understanding of materials and by precision engineering in wood and metal; and by an ear which knows the difference between a pretentious noise and a sound with musical potential. This constant faithfulness to the highest technical standards may then be modified by that educated instinct which musicians call 'bon goût' and instrument makers refer to as 'rule of thumb'. Thus is music the mistress of the builder's craft.

Dom Bédos' text to his plate LII (which provides a detailed 'view of an organ as if cut vertically at the centre, seen from the side') is therefore as instructive today—and as illustrative of the instrument's complexities—as it was in the eighteenth century; save only that the bellows-boy, by and large, has been replaced by an electric fan. It is therefore worth reprinting here (in a translation by Charles Ferguson) as a supplement to Chapter 2. Passages contained within brackets are editorial.

Half the *Positif* case [a *Positif á dos*], with a large number of pipes, is shown at 2. The main case is labelled 3. The organist is shown at 4, seated at the console and playing. His fingers touch the manuals, 6, his left foot touches a pedal, 7, and his right foot rests on the iron rail [provided for a temporarily resting foot, and to help the player keep his balance]. He sits on bench 8. The bellows-boy is labelled 5; he is operating the bellows, 9, by pulling down levers 10, 11, and 12 attached to bellows 13, 14, and 15. The wind generated by the bellows enters the trunk, 40, whose end is open because it is cut away. In reality, this trunk is considerably longer and connects with several more bellows. From trunk 40 the wind enters the light tremulant [*tremblant doux*], 17, through trunk 16. From the tremulant box, it divides and passes to two destinations: the pallet-box of the *Grand orgue* chest, 19, through trunk 18; and the pallet-box of the *Positif*, 21, through trunk 20. The *Grand orgue* pallet-boxes supply wind to the *Pédale* chest, 37, by means of a trunk which is plainly to be seen.

The four manuals are labelled 6, sectioned through the centre so as to show their main components: the back-rails with grooves to receive the key-tails, the centre-rails which limit the dip of the keys, the pull-downs, the guide-rail for the stickers to the *Positif*, and the knee-board which protects and hides the pedal action. This panel is shown fitted into dadoes at the top and bottom, which is an error. It must be mounted in a rabbet only, so that it may be removed. [The term dado here refers to a groove, while a rabbet is a step-shaped channel into which the panel fits.]

Since the pedalboard is likewise sectioned, the heads [front ends] of the pedals are shown with the trackers connected, the rail which limits the dip of the pedals, the back-rail with the groove in which the tails of the pedals fit, and the board through which the pedals extend from beneath.

Below the pedalboard, the backfalls for the *Positif*, 23, can be seen, as well as the stickers, 24, whose upper ends support the keys of the *Positif* manual; their lower ends stand on the ends of the backfalls, which in turn pivot on rail 25. The opposite ends of the backfalls, 27, extend under the *Positif* chest, 21, 26, 28, 27. Since the chest is sectioned, the following elements can be observed: the interior of the pallet-box, 21; the latch-irons; the pallet-spring guide; the pallets; the small stickers, 28, covered by purses, resting on the ends of the backfalls; and the bars of the chest: one is labelled 28, 26. There may also be seen sections of the table [on which the pipes stand], sliders, spacers, toe-boards [which receive the pipefeet], and rack-boards [which hold the pipes upright], as well as a number of pipes. The false floor built between the main case and the *Positif*, to protect the backfalls and support the pedalboard, is labelled 30, 29, 21.

Note the trackers, 31, connected to the manual pull-downs below, and above to the arms of the roller-board, 32. The rollers are seen in cross-section. Within the *Grand orgue* pallet-box, 19, are seen the pallets, and below them the pull-downs, connected to trackers from rollerboard 32. The *Grand orgue* chest, 19, is fitted with sliders, toe-boards, rack-boards, etc., and a maze of pipework, 3.

The pedals, 7, pull down trackers 38, turning the squares [right-angle connectors] of rail 33. This motion is relayed to square-rail 34 by trackers, and by means of other trackers 39, the squares in rail 35 pull the diagonal trackers connected to rollerboard 36 for *Pédale* chest 37, whose pallets are thus opened. At the open pallet-box of this chest are seen the pallets, pull-downs, and corresponding trackers. Above the chest are seen the rack-board and portions of pipes.

It will be observed, finally, that the first key shown in the *Positif* manual is depressed by the organist's left little finger. The sticker, 24, is thereby lowered, and it rocks backfall 23, 27 so as to raise the end which lies under the chest. This motion is imparted to sticker 28 and opens the pallet, as shown.

The heavy tremulant [*tremblant fort*], 22, is mounted on windtrunk 18. The drawstop action has been omitted from this plate, to make clearer the manual and pedal actions and the wind supply.

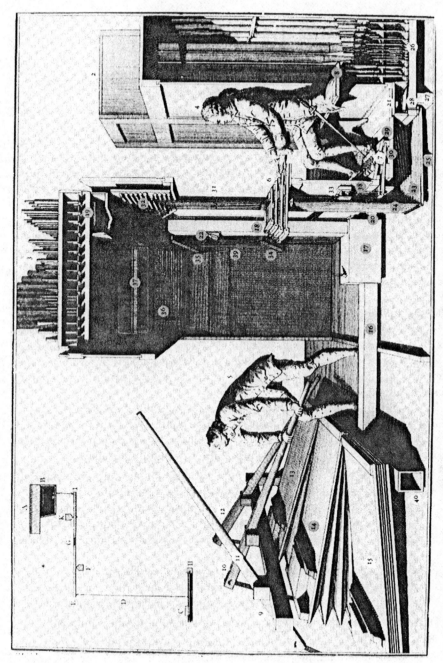

François Bédos de Celles, *L'Art du Facteur d'Orgues* (Paris, 1766–78), plate LII, in the Library of the Royal College of Organists (*photo* John D. Sharp).

APPENDIX II: THE 'SWELL-BOX'

By the middle of the seventeenth century, most new French organs of serious pretensions possessed Grand Orgue and Positif divisions of 48 notes each (CD–c³), and two short-compass divisions (usually 25 notes from c¹), one for right-hand solos (Récit) and the other playing the Echo pipes. These were placed deep inside the instrument, under the Grand Orgue. The idea of an enclosed division proved popular and by the beginning of the eighteenth century Echo organs were becoming common also in Spain and England. The large organ in Seville Cathedral (1673) had its Oberwerk converted to a swell-box in 1703. At the Temple Church in London (1688) the Ecchos was totally enclosed in a wooden box. Renatus Harris claimed to have made an expressive box (probably by lifting its lid) for his organ for Salisbury Cathedral in 1710, and Abraham Jordan certainly made a box, the front of which had a sliding shutter and a pedal to control it, for a London church in 1712. By the second half of the eighteenth century the conversion of Echo boxes was providing good work for English organ-builders, and by the beginning of the next century the Swell division was beginning to replace the 'Chair' organ as the secondary manual to the Great.

During the nineteenth century the gradual whittling away of articulative control in key-touch was balanced in expressive terms by a more sophisticated use of the swell-box. By the 1850s, the combination of rich 16′ 8′ 4′ reeds and a flue chorus culminating in scintillating mixture-work had established the Swell as a powerfully expressive and uniquely English development. The best effect has always come from shallow boxes backed by a stone wall.

The musical use of the swell-box shutters—as with all expressive devices—is ultimately a reflection of the performer's good taste, and the player who 'pumps' the swell pedal regardless of the musical context or of phrasing is still all too common, even today. Legitimate use of the 'expression pedal' may well include the following:

   (i) phrases in Romantic and modern music marked with 'hairpin' crescendo and dimuendo signs; the horizontal box shutters on most nineteenth-century organs resembled Venetian-blinds, and were controlled by foot pedals capable at best only of three positions (closed, half-closed, and open): infinite gradations of volume (later feasible with twentieth-century balanced vertical shutters) were only possible given strong leg muscles!

  (ii) dynamic accents, involving sudden movements of the shutters;

 (iii) achieving a balance between two or more divisions of the organ before the performance starts—useful in all periods of music, including baroque.

The principal drawbacks of expression boxes may be summarized as follows:

   (i) whether the box is open or closed, a certain attenuation of pipe consonants, resulting in less clear projection in quick contrapuntal music; the deeper the box (from front shutters to the back) the more marked will be this effect;

(ii) when the box is *completely* closed, a marked lack of projection and an increased tendency for melodic notes apparently to overlap; for this reason, it is advisable usually to leave the shutters very slightly open, except at cadences, or in music where a distant harmonic effect is required;

(iii) a subjective flattening of pitch as the shutters begin to open, especially when 8′ stops alone are used; this is another reason to consider leaving the shutters very slightly open. 'The uncertainty of pitch of a choir or congregation which is being accompanied on a swell organ, with much swell-pedalling, is well known, and is cured as soon as the organist transfers his hands to the bright tone of an unenclosed [division]';[1] and on the subject of accompaniment, there is little need to remind the hymn-playing organist of the disastrous effect on lusty, congregational singing if he drops suddenly from full Great to 'full swell with the box shut'—grown men can be stopped dead in their tracks, and vengeance sworn!

[1] Sumner, *The Organ*, p. 271.

APPENDIX III: A BRIEF EXPLANATION OF TEMPERAMENT IN KEYBOARD TUNING

Most people know that the vibrations of a high-pitched note are faster than that of a low note, and are aware that frequency doubles for every octave ascended—a fact which is inversely mirrored in the phenomenon that the sounding length of an organ-pipe halves, roughly speaking, for every octave ascended. The frequency ratio of an octave is said to be $2:1$. Other natural (acoustically true) intervals also have simple frequency ratios:

Fifth	$3:2$
Fourth	$4:3$
Major third	$5:4$
Minor third	$6:5$

However, when we try to extend these formulae, we find that 12 perfect fifths are slightly *larger* than 7 octaves (starting from a low C and ascending by true fifths, we come after 12 steps to a B♯ which is sharper than C). But worse is to come, since three pure thirds are slightly *smaller* than an octave (B♯ is this time flatter than C). Mathematically speaking

$$\text{three thirds} = \tfrac{5}{4} \times \tfrac{5}{4} \times \tfrac{5}{4} \left(\tfrac{125}{64}\right) \text{ whereas the octave} = \tfrac{2}{1} \left(\tfrac{128}{64}\right)$$

As octaves must always be in true relationship, it is evident that some of the fifths and thirds must submit to some minute adjustment. Singers, and string and wind players do this for themselves to a large extent, but for a keyboard instrument with only twelve possibilities per octave a system is necessary. The way in which this adjustment is made is called *temperament*, and has varied from period to period. If we want to savour exactly how a composer would have expected his music to sound when he wrote it, some experience of various temperaments is a great help. (Organ builders are increasingly becoming aware of the advantages of tuning some organs in systems other than equal temperament.)

Historically, the first temperament of interest to organists is *mean-tone*, which became widespread in the sixteenth century but survived in organs longer than in other instruments, because of the trouble and expense of altering organ-pipes. The salient characteristic of mean-tone is that the thirds in the commonly used keys are pure, though this is achieved by making all the fifths in the octave, except one, noticeably small. (The remaining fifth, the famous howling 'wolf', is unusably large.) In the simple keys, this temperament has the benefit of beautiful serene-sounding major triads, though remoter keys give much more inharmonious triads which lure the wolf from its lair! Another characteristic of mean-tone is that, because of the way in which the fifths are spaced, the semitones are notably unequal; chromatic semitones (e.g. F-F♯) are smaller than diatonic ones (e.g. F♯-G). This gives a remarkable expressive character to chromatic melodies, and has the further effect—to our equally-tempered ears—of making the leading-notes of keys such as G, D, or A sound notably flat. It is a temperament which takes some getting used to, but grants many insights once its point is understood.

One should note that in mean-tone the accidentals were tuned as F♯, C♯, G♯, B♭, and E♭—*not* their enharmonic equivalents—and this imposed natural limitations of chording and tonality. But such limitations became increasingly irksome, and the later Baroque period was notable for many efforts to develop more adaptable temperaments. The *well-tempered* systems proposed by Werckmeister and Kirnberger were typical. Such temperaments rest upon a different compromise, distributing the impossible 'wolf' fifth of mean-tone between four, five, or six of the fifths in the scale, and leaving the other fifths pure. This gives rise to thirds of various sizes, ranging from pure (that is, smaller than equal temperament) to ones rather inharmoniously large. The way in which the thirds are arranged in this kind of system results in a perceptible difference between keys, but all keys are at least usable. Scholars are now agreed that it was for some such system that Bach wrote his 'Well-Tempered' (though not equally-tempered!) 48 preludes and fugues. As far as the organ is concerned, there is evidence that certain organs may have been tuned in these temperaments by 1700—for instance, that of the Marienkirche in Lübeck, thus making possible the famous F♯ minor Praeludium of Buxtehude. Bach himself must have been accustomed to writing in a well-tempered system by the time of the Orgel-Büchlein: 'Ich ruf' zu dir' would be very sour in mean-tone tuning.

Equal temperament was slow to be accepted for organs; not a single organ at the Great Exhibition in London in 1851 was tuned thus. This is hardly surprising, since mixtures (whose ranks are tuned in pure intervals) tend to sound better in temperaments which have at least some pure fifths in their scale. Furthermore, to those musicians and listeners used to the timbres and harmonic subtleties of the various tempered systems, the new method must have seemed to lack colour and sparkle, and indeed to have lost a whole dimension. Equal temperament has no acoustically true intervals except for the octave, and its advantages in terms of modulatory adventurousness are balanced—some might say negated—by the lack of that spice and agreeable argument to be found between the simple keys and their more daring neighbours.

The organ is an instrument well known for its sensitivity to even the smallest alterations of tuning, due to its characteristic lack of a 'dying fall' (explained on p. 8) and its use of stops based on the partials of the harmonic series. It is now a (usually) happy hunting ground for practitioners of historical temperament; the most commonly encountered systems are those of Werckmeister III (1691) and Vallotti (1754). The new Fisk organ in Stanford, USA, has an ingenious system of 17 pipes to the octave, which enables either mean-tone or well-tempered tuning to be selected at the touch of a lever. Harald Vogel has recorded Bach's 'Das alte Jahr' chorale prelude on this organ in both

APPENDIX IV: SPECIFICATIONS OF ORGANS

S. Giuseppe, Brescia (1581)

Organ by Graziado Antegnati. A single-manual organ with pedal pull-downs. The compass was 53 notes from CC (an octave below today's lowest note) to a^2, though there were no sharps below AA, and no g$\sharp^2$. The pitch was about a semitone above the modern standard.

	Today's pitch at C
Principale	8′ (divided)
Ottava	4′
Quintadecima	2′
Decimanona	1$\frac{1}{3}$′
Vigesimaseconda	1′
Vigesimasesta	$\frac{2}{3}$′
Vigesimanona	$\frac{1}{2}$′
Trigesimaterza	$\frac{1}{3}$′
Trigesimasesta	$\frac{1}{4}$′
Flauto in ottava	4′
Flauto in duodecima	2$\frac{2}{3}$′
Flauto in quintadecima	2′
Fiffaro	8′ (treble pipes only)

The music of Frescobaldi (1583-1643) was written for an organ such as this, soft-toned and gentle, without reeds.[1] Williams points out that 'the downward compass of such Italian organs ideally varied with the size of the church: the larger the church, the longer the bass compass'.[2]

Marienkirche, Lübeck

During Buxtehude's long tenure (over thirty-five years) the larger of the church's two organs was modernized by various additions and some rebuilding, resulting in the

---

[1] Costanzo Antegnati (son of Graziado) wrote an important treatise on the organ of his time (*L'Arte Organica*, Brescia, 1608). His rules for using contemporary organ registration are quoted by P.-G. Andersen (see Reading List); see also Peter Williams, *The European Organ (1450-1850)* (Batsford: London, 1966), ch. 6.

[2] *A New History of the Organ: From the Greeks to the Present Day* (Faber & Faber: London, 1980), p. 84.

following specification; the organ was replaced with one by Schulze in the middle of the nineteenth century.

Hauptwerk		Stuhlpositiv (Rückpositiv)		Brustwerk		Pedal	
Prinzipal	16′	Bordun	16′	Prinzipal	8′	Prinzipal	32′
Quintadena	16′	Prinzipal	8′	Gedackt	8′	Oktav	16′
Octav	8′	Rohrflöte	8′	Oktav	4′	Subbass	16′
Spitzflöte	8′	Quintatön	8′	Rohrflöte	4′	Oktav	8′
Oktav	4′	Oktav	4′	Nachthorn	2′	Gedackt	8′
Rohrflöte	4′	Blockflöte	4′	Schweitserpfeife	2′	Oktav	4′
Nasat	2⅔′	Spillflöte	2′	Sifflöte	1⅓′	Nachthorn	2′
Rauschpfeife II	—	Sesquialtera II	—	Sesquialtera II	—	Bauernflöte	1′
Mixtur X–XV	—	Mixtur V	—	Mixtur VI–VIII	—	Mixtur VI	—
Scharff IV	—	Scharff IV–V	—	Zimbel III	—	Posaune	24′
Trompete	16′	Dulcian	16′	Krummhorn	8′	Posaune	16′
Trompete	8′	Trichterregal	8′	Regal	8′	Dulcian	16′
Zinck	4′	Barpfeiffe	8′			Trompete	8′
		Vox humana	8′			Krummhorn	8′
						Cornett	2′

Inter-manual couplers; two Tremulants; two Drums; Cimbelstern

The smaller organ in the Totentanz chapel, destroyed in 1942, was a superb example of the evolution of a *Werkprinzip* organ over a 150-year period:

Hauptwerk (Begun, 1476–7)		Rückpositiv (1557–8)		Brustwerk (1621–2)		Pedal (1475–7, 1621–2)	
Quintade	16′	Prinzipal	8′	Gedackt	8′	Prinzipal	16′
Prinzipal	8′	Rohrflöte	8′	Quintade	4′	Subbass	16′
Spitzflöte	8′	Quintatön	8′	Hohlflöte	2′	Oktav	8′
Oktav	4′	Oktav	4′	Quintflöte	1⅓′	Gedackt	8′
Nasat	2⅔′	Rohrflöte	4′	Scharff IV	—	Oktav	4′
Rauschpfeife II	—	Sesquialtera II	—	Krummhorn	8′	Quintade	4′
Mixtur VIII–X	—	Sifflöte	1⅓′	Schalmei	4′	Oktav	2′
Trompete	8′	Scharff VI–VIII	—			Nachthorn	1′ (1937)
		Dulzian	16′			Mixtur IV	—
Rückpositiv/		Trichterregal	8′			Zimbel II	—
Hauptwerk(1760)						Posaune	16′
						Dulcian	16′ (1760)
						Trompete	8′
						Schalmei	4′
						Cornett	2′
						(removed in 1760)	

Weimar Castle Chapel

J. S. Bach wrote much of his organ music during his time at Weimar (1708–17), including, for example, the *Orgel-Büchlein*. The organ was situated in the highest gallery of this
very tall chapel. The entire castle was burned down in the nineteenth century.

Hauptwerk		Positiv		Pedal	
Quintaton	16′	Prinzipal	8′	Gross Untersatz	32′
Prinzipal	8′	Gedackt	8′	Violonbass	16′
Gemshorn	8′	Viola di gamba	8′	Subbass	16′
Gedackt	8′	Oktav	4′	Prinzipalbass	8′
Oktav	4′	Kleingedackt	4′	Posaune	16′
Quintaton	4′	Waldflöte	2′	Trompeten bass	8′
Mixtur VI	—	Sesquialtera II	—	Cornetten bass	4′
Cymbel III	—	Trompete	8′		
Glockenspiel		Tremulant			
Tremulant					
Positiv/Hauptwerk		Cymbelstern		Hauptwerk/Pedal	

St Blasius, Mühlhausen

Organ as reconstructed to specifications by J. S. Bach (1709). The compass of the
manuals was C–d³, and pedals C–d¹; there was no bottom C♯.

Hauptwerk		Rückpositiv	
Quintadena	16′	Quintatön	8′
Prinzipal	8′	Gedackt	8′
*Viola da Gamba	8′	Prinzipal	4′
Oktave	4′	Salizional	4′
Gedackt	4′	Oktave	2′
*Nasat	2⅔′	Spitzflöte	2′
Oktave	2′	Quintflöte	1⅓′
Sesquialtera II	—	Sesquialtera II	—
Mixtur IV	—	Zimbel III	—
Zimbel II	—		
*Fagott	16′		

Brustwerk		Pedal	
*Stillgedackt (wood)	8′	*Untersatz	32′
*Flauto dolce	4′	Prinzipal	16′
*Quinte	2⅔′	Subbass	16′
*Prinzipal	2′	Oktave	8′
*Terz	1⅗′	Oktave	4′
*Mixtur III	—	Rohrflöte	1′
*Schalmei	8′	Mixtur IV	—
		Posaune	16′
*Brustwerk/Hauptwerk		Trompete	8′
Ruckpositiv/Hauptwerk		Cornett	2′
Hauptwerk/Pedal		Glockenspiel	4′

One Tremulant (acting on all manuals)

Zimbelstern
Pauke

New stops specified by Bach are marked *. On the *Hauptwerk*, the Viola, Nasat, and Fagott replaced respectively a Gemshorn 8′, Quinte 2⅔′, and Trompete 8′. Points worthy of especial note are the inclusion of a Sesquialtera sound (2⅔′, 1⅗′) on each manual; the *Brustwerk* (which was an entirely new division, to Bach's design, on which the 8′ and 4′ flutes were very quiet, and well suited to continuo playing); the 32′ Untersatz (which gives the whole organ 'die beste Gravität'); the 16′ Fagott[3] ('which is useful for all kinds of new ideas, and sounds very fine in concerted music');[4] and the Tremulant (which Bach wished to be carefully regulated to wave the tone properly). In addition, Bach asked for new resonators, so that the Posaune might match the *Gravität* of the new 32′. The Glockenspiel was included at the behest of the parishioners; Bach's personal opinion is not known.

Ponitz

The organ of this Saxony village church, built 1734-7 and recently restored, is one of Gottfried Silbermann's finest extant instruments. Its design is typical of his village church organs—around 20-8 stops divided between two manual divisions (their chests placed one above the other, or side-by-side) and a small pedal department, all contained within a box-like non-freestanding case on the west wall of the gallery. The compass of the manuals is 48 notes (C-c³), and of the pedals 24 notes (C-c¹); bottom C♯ is omitted. The manual divisions are designed as equal partners, while the pedal offers simply a strong or gentle bass line—contrary to the more developed pedal of seventeenth-century

[3] See Peter Williams, *The Organ Music of J. S. Bach*, Vol. 2, p. 262, regarding Sesquialtera and Fagotto registrations in BWV 720.

[4] Bach's memorandum, Eng. trans. in David and Mendel, eds., *The Bach reader*, pp. 58-60.

Saxony. The tonal character of Gottfried Silbermann's organs combines the French influences of his early years (from working with his brother, Andreas, in Alsace) with the earlier Saxony style. The resulting sound—at once strong, clear, and lustrous—and the variety of colour obtainable from so few stops, constantly excites and challenges both player and listener. Among such organs, a handful can offer to music-making that rare, extra spiritual dimension which is a characteristic only of the greatest musical instruments. The organs of this builder are also important because of their proximity to J. S. Bach, both in date of construction and geographical location during Bach's 27 years in Leipzig from 1723. In the light of their tonal style, questions must arise as to whether they could have influenced Bach's registrational ideas for works written in this period, especially *Clavier-Übung III* (1739), and how Bach, in performance, might have dealt with the musical limitations of organs with this type of pedal specification and compass (for most of his organ works—the majority written by 1717—envisage a pedalboard including at least pedal d^1: see Mühlhausen specification, p. 149.

Hauptwerk		*Oberwerk*		*Pedal*	
Bordun	16	Principal	8	Principal-Bass	16
Principal	8	Gedackt	8	Octav-Bass	8
Rohr-Flöthe	8	Quintadehn	8	Posaunen-Bass	16
Viol di Gamba	8	Octava	4		
Octava	4	Rohr-Flöthe	4		
Spitz-Flöthe	4	Nassat	3		
Quinta	3	Octava	2		
Octava	2	Gemshorn	2		
Tertia	1$\frac{3}{5}$	Sesquialtera	1$\frac{3}{5}$		
Mixtur IV	—	Quinta	1$\frac{1}{2}$		
Cornett III	—	Siffloeth	1		
		Cymbeln II	—		
		Vox Humana	8		

Manualschiebe-Koppel*
Tremulant (Hw)
Schwebung (Ow)

In 1884, a Manual/Pedal coupler was added. The organ also possesses a Glockenspiel which was added in 1872. It is tuned in equal temperament, and the pitch at a^1 is 463 Hz at 15 °C.

* The manuals are coupled by sliding the upper keyboard partly over the lower one, so that their actions interconnect.

The Temple Church, London

English organs had no pedals at all until the late eighteenth century. 'Even in the second decade of the nineteenth century only nine of thirty-three cathedral and abbey organs in Britain had pedals, and in all but two of these cases they were pull-downs acting on the

Great organ keys'.[5] Yet some organs were nevertheless quite large instruments. The organs installed by 'Father' Bernard Smith in the Temple Church in 1688 possessed three divisions, Great, Choir, and Ecchos. Forty-two years later, Christopher Schrider (Smith's son-in-law) made a swell-box out of the totally enclosed Ecchos by installing a shutter. In 1741 (by which time John Stanley had been one of the organists at the Temple Church for seven years) John Byfield added a new Swell containing six stops of short compass, in the manner of a French *Récit*.

The compass of Smith's organ is given below, together with his stop-list for the instrument. Where indicated (└──┘), D♯ and G♯ were divided (the rear part of the black keys being on separate action and raised above the front part) to give the option of playing E♭ and A♭. This enabled the mean-tone temperament of the time to accommodate modulatory devices which would otherwise have sounded excessively discordant. The total compass of the organ was therefore 61 notes.

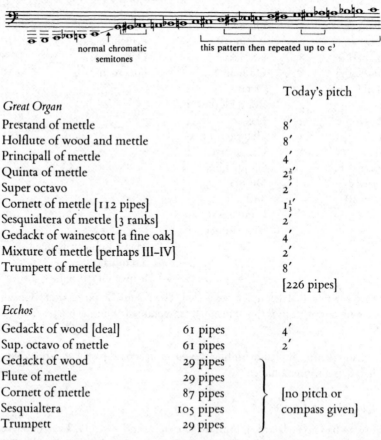

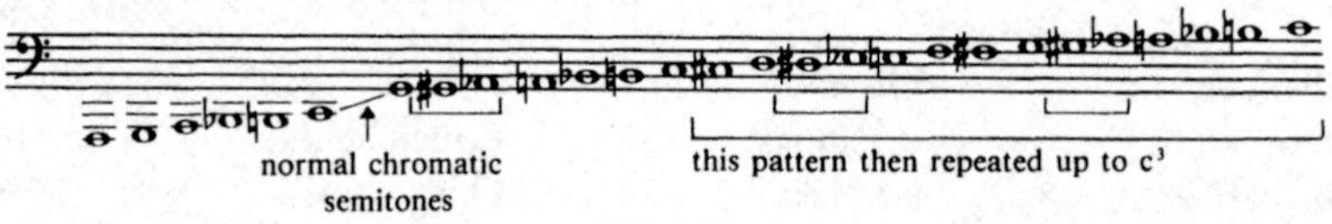
normal chromatic
semitones
this pattern then repeated up to c³

		Today's pitch
Great Organ		
Prestand of mettle		8′
Holflute of wood and mettle		8′
Principall of mettle		4′
Quinta of mettle		$2\frac{2}{3}'$
Super octavo		2′
Cornett of mettle [112 pipes]		$1\frac{1}{3}'$
Sesquialtera of mettle [3 ranks]		2′
Gedackt of wainescott [a fine oak]		4′
Mixture of mettle [perhaps III–IV]		2′
Trumpett of mettle		8′
		[226 pipes]
Ecchos		
Gedackt of wood [deal]	61 pipes	4′
Sup. octavo of mettle	61 pipes	2′
Gedackt of wood	29 pipes	[no pitch or compass given]
Flute of mettle	29 pipes	
Cornett of mettle	87 pipes	
Sesquialtera	105 pipes	
Trumpett	29 pipes	

[5] William L. Sumner, *The Organ: Its Evolution, Principles of Construction and Use* (MacDonald: London, 1952), p. 175.

Choir Organ

Gedackt of wainescott	8′
Holflute of mettle	4′
A Sadt [possibly Gemshorn] of mettle	4′
Spitts flute of mettle	2′
A Violl and Violin of mettle	8′
Voice humane of mettle[6]	8′

New Swell added by Byfield in 1741:

Open diapason
Stopped diapason
Cornet, 4 ranks
Horn
Trumpet
Hautbois

Compass g–c³, except for the Horn (f–c³)

St Gervais, Paris

This was François Couperin's organ in 1685/6 when his appointment as organist was confirmed. In 1685, Alexandre Thierry had raised the organ's pitch about one semitone, bringing it to about a semitone under today's average standard.[7]

Grand orgue (49 notes C–c³)

Montre	16′
Bourdon	16′
Montre	8′
Bourdon	8′
Prestant	4′
Flûte	4′
Nazard	2⅔′
Doublette	2′
Quarte	2′
Tierce	1⅗′
Fourniture IV	—
Cymbale III	—
Cornet V (25 notes)	—
Trompette	8′

Positif (49 notes)

Bourdon	8′
Montre	4′
Flûte	4′
Nazard	2⅔′
Doublette	2′
Tierce	1⅗′
Larigot	1⅓′
Fourniture III	—
Cymbale III	—
Chromhorne	8′

Echo (37 notes)

Bourdon	8′
Prestant	4′

[over]

---

[6] '. . . set to Mr Gascell's voice, who can reach one of the deepest basses in England' (from an anonymous manuscript notebook in the Middle Temple Library).

[7] Specification borrowed from *Oeuvres Complètes de François Couperin*, Vol. III, *Pièces d'Orgue*, revised edition K. Gilbert and D. Moroney (Éditions de L'Oiseau-Lyre: Monaco, 1982).

Grand orgue (49 notes C–c³)

Voix humaine	8′
Clairon	4′
Tremblant fort	
Tremblant doux	

Récit (25 notes)

Cornet V	—

Écho (37 notes)

Nazard	$2\frac{2}{3}′$
Doublette	2′
Tierce	$1\frac{3}{5}′$
Cymbale III	—
Chromhorne	8′

Pédale (29 notes)

Flûte	8′
Flûte	4′
Trompette	8′

Tirasse (coupler)
Grand orgue/Pédale

On the *Grand Orgue*, *Positif*, and *Pédale*, bottom C♯ played the A below.

Ste Clotilde, Paris

César Franck's organ, built by Cavaillé-Coll in 1859. It was subsequently rebuilt in 1933 and 1962.

Grand Orgue

Montre	16′
Bourdon	16′
Montre	8′
Flûte harmonique	8′
Bourdon	8′
Viole de Gambe	8′
Prestant	4′
Flûte octaviante	4′
Quinte	$2\frac{2}{3}′$
Doublette	2′
Plein jeu harmonique VII	—
Bombarde	16′
Trompette	8′
Clairon	4′

Positif

Bourdon	16′
Montre	8′
Flûte harmonique	8′
Bourdon	8′
Gambe	8′
Unda maris	8′
Prestant	4′
Flûte octaviante	4′
Quint	$2\frac{2}{3}′$
Doublette	2′
Plein jeu IV	—
Trompette	8′
Clairon	4′
Clarinette	8′

Récit (expressif)

Bourdon	8′
Flûte harmonique	8′

Pédale

Soubasse	32′
Contrebasse	16′

Récit (expressif)		*Pédale*	
Viole de Gambe	8′	Basse	8′
Voix Céleste	8′	Octave	4′
Basson-Hautbois	8′	⌠ Bombarde	16′
Voix humaine	8′	⎪ Basson	16′
⌠ Flûte octaviante	4′	⎨ Trompette	8′
⎪ Octavin	2′	⎩ Clairon	4′
⎨ Trompette	8′		
⎩ Clairon	4′		

Tremblant

The compass of the manuals was C–f³ (54 notes), and of the Pedals C–d¹ (27 notes). The order of the manuals (top to bottom) was *Récit*, *Positif*, *Grand Orgue*.

Situated in a row immediately above the keys of the pedalboard, and within comfortable reach of the organist's toes, were twelve iron hitch-down pedals, controlling:

1.	*Tirasses—Grand Orgue*	Manual to Pedal couplers.
2.	*—Positif*	
3.	*Anches Pédale*	see *Appel d'anches*, below.
4.	*Octaves graves—Grand Orgue*	Sub-octave coupling on
5.	*—Positif*	the *Grand Orgue* and
6.	*—Récit/Positif*	*Positif*, and on the *Récit* when coupled to and played on the *Positif* manual.
7.	*Anches—Grand Orgue*	*Appel d'anches* shut off
8.	*—Positif*	the wind supply to any stops
9.	*—Récit*	drawn in those sections bracketed in the stop-list, allowing registration to be prepared in advance.
10.	*Accouplements—Positif/Grand Orgue*	Intermanual couplers. Although there was no
11.	*—Récit/Positif*	*Récit/Grand Orgue* coupler, the *Récit* could be coupled to the *Grand Orgue* via the *Positif*.
12.	Tremulant	

The *boîte d'expression* was a hitch-down pedal controlling the opening and closing of the *Récit* shutters.

READING LIST

* Author's choice of sixteen books to form the core of a library for the intending performer.

*ANDERSEN, PAUL-GERHARD, *Orgelbogen* (Munksgaard, Copenhagen, 1956); trans. J. Curnutt as *Organ Building and Design* (Allen and Unwin: London, 1969). Represents the minimum technical information on organ design that an organist should know. Very readable.

ANTHONY, JAMES R., *French Baroque Music from Beaujoyeulx to Rameau* (2nd edn., Batsford: London, 1978). Chapter 18 deals briefly with organ music of the *grand siècle*.

*BACH, C. P. E., *Versuch über die wahre Art das Clavier zu spielen* (Berlin, 1753); trans. W. J. Mitchell as *Essay on the True Art of Playing Keyboard Instruments* (Eulenburg: London, 1974).

BROWN, HOWARD MAYER, *Embellishing 16th-Century Music* (Oxford University Press: London, 1976).

—— 'Performing Practice', *The New Grove Dictionary* (Macmillan: London, 1980), Vol. 14, p. 370.

BUCK, PERCY C., *Psychology for Musicians* (Oxford University Press: London, 1944).

CAVAILLÉ-COLL, ARISTIDE, *Complete Theoretical Works* ed.and annotated by G. Huybens, Bibliotheca Organologica 41 (Fritz Knuf: Buren, Netherlands, 1978). Introd. in English, all texts in French.

CLUTTON, CECIL, and NILAND, AUSTIN, *The British Organ* (rev. and enlarged, Eyre Methuen: London, 1981).

CONE, EDWARD T., *Musical Form and Musical Performance* (Norton: New York, 1968).

*COPLAND, AARON, *What to Listen for in Music* (McGraw-Hill: New York and London, 1957). A book for listeners that all musicians should read.

COUPERIN, FRANÇOIS, *L'art de toucher le clavecin* (Paris, 1716). French text with parallel Germ. and Eng. trans. by Anna Linde (Breitkopf & Härtel: Wiesbaden, 1933; repr. 1961).

*DART, THURSTON, *The Interpretation of Music* (4th edn., Hutchinson: London, 1967). A classic for every performer's library.

DAVID, H. T., and MENDEL, A., *The Bach Reader: A Life of Johann Sebastian Bach in Letters and Documents* (Norton: New York, 1945). A fascinating compendium of documents and eighteenth-century commentary on Bach the man and the musician.

DOLMETSCH, ARNOLD, *The Interpretation of the Music of the XVIIth and XVIIIth Centuries* (London, 1915). As revealed by contemporary evidence and introd. by Alec Harman. (Repr., Washington University Press: Washington, 1969).

DONINGTON, ROBERT, *A Performer's Guide to Baroque Music* (Faber and Faber: London, 1973). Shares some material with his *The Interpretation of Early Music*, but is more extensive on certain aspects, e.g. bel canto voice-production and accidentals.

—— *The Interpretation of Early Music* (New version, Faber and Faber: London, 1974). Very detailed.

—— *Baroque Music: Style and Performance* (Faber and Faber: London, 1982). A valuable handbook, in paperback.

*DOUGLASS, FENNER, *The Language of the Classical French Organ* (Yale University Press: New Haven, 1969). A classic and detailed background book.

DOWNES, RALPH, *Baroque Tricks: Adventures with the Organ Builders* (Positif Press: Oxford, 1983). For anyone interested in the English organ renaissance of the past forty years; very readable.

*EMERY, WALTER, *Bach's Ornaments* (Novello: London, 1953). Still the most useful specialist handbook; detailed yet thought-provoking.

—— *Notes on Bach's Organ Works: Six Sonatas for 3 Manuals and Pedal* (Novello: London, 1957). Accompanies Emery's Novello edition of the sonatas.

*FERGUSON, HOWARD, *Keyboard Interpretation* (Oxford University Press: London, 1975). Mainly concerned with stringed keyboard instruments and their music. Problems involved with music intended exclusively for the organ are not discussed, but nevertheless a useful background handbook for any keyboardist.

FESPERMAN, JOHN, *The Organ as Musical Medium* (Coleman-Ross: Boston, 1962). '. . . an attempt to develop an understanding of the organ as an appropriate and distinctive means for making music.'

—— *Two Essays on Organ Design* (Sunbury, 1975).

FORSYTH-GRANT, MAURICE I., *Twenty-One Years of Organ-Building* (Positif Press: Oxford, 1987). By the man who brought the uncompromising classical organ to English organ-building.

GRIFFITHS, PAUL, *Olivier Messiaen and the Music of Time* (Faber and Faber: London, 1985). Includes searching analyses and discussions of all the major works, suggesting how they function as works of art and not only as theological symbols.

GRINDEA, CAROLA, *Tensions in the Performance of Music: A Symposium* (Kahn & Averill: London, 1978). Explores the problems of physical tension in performing music.

HAMILTON, JOHN, 'An emerging U. S. Organ-building Movement', *Musical Times* 125 (June and July 1984).

HARMON, THOMAS, *The Registration of J. S. Bach's Organ Works*, Bibliotheca Organologica 70 (Fritz Knuf: Buren, Netherlands, 1978).

HIGGINBOTTOM, EDWARD, 'French Classical Organ Music and the Liturgy', *Proceedings of the Royal Musical Association* 103 (1976).

—— *An Introduction to French Classical Organ Music*, 4 vols. (Novello: London, forthcoming).

HOPKINS, E. J., and RIMBAULT, E. F., *The Organ, its History and Construction*, Bibliotheca Organologica 4 (Fritz Knuf: Buren, Netherlands, 1981). Reprint of 1877 edition; a classic of its period.

IRWIN, STEVENS, *Dictionary of Pipe Organ Stops* (2nd edn., Collier Macmillan: London, 1983).

JACOBSON, LENA, 'Musical Rhetoric in Buxtehude's Free Organ Works', *Organ Year Book* 13 (1982), p. 60.

KARSTÄDT, GEORG, *Buxtehude-Werke-Verzeichnis* (BuxWV) (Breitkopf & Härtel, Wiesbaden, 1974). Thematic index of Buxtehude's works.

KELLER, HERMANN, *Phrasierung und Artikulation* (Kassel, 1955); Eng. trans. as *Phrasing and Articulation* (Hutchinson: London, 1965).

*—— *Die Orgelwerke Bachs* (Leipzig, 1948); Eng. trans. H. Hewitt as *The Organ Works of Bach* (Peters: London, 1967). Written 'by a musician and for musicians. It is the result of an earnest effort to understand Bach's organ works: their inner logic, their form ... interpretation ... performance.' Should be read, if not owned, by every serious organ student.

KIRKPATRICK, RALPH, 'On Re-reading Couperin's *L'Art de toucher le clavecin*' *Early Music* 4 (1976), No. 1, p. 3.

KLOPPERS, JACOBUS, 'A Criterion for Manual Changes in the Organ Works of Bach', *Organ Year Book* 7 (1976), p. 59.

LE HURAY, PETER, 'Fingering', in *The New Grove Dictionary* (Macmillan: London, 1980), Vol. 6, p. 567.

*—— 'English Keyboard Fingering in the 16th and early 17th Centuries', *Source Materials and the Interpretation of Music*, ed. Ian Bent (Stainer and Bell: London, 1981).

—— *The Spirit of Authenticity: Case Studies in Eighteenth-Century Performance Practice* (Cambridge University Press: Cambridge, 1990). What are the central issues that confront the performer of high-baroque and 'classical' music? The discussion is focused on nine well-known works that span a broad cross-section of eighteenth-century idioms, including the Passacaglia (BWV 582).

—— and BUTT, JOHN, 'In Search of Bach the Organist', *Bach, Handel and Scarlatti*, ed. Peter Williams (Cambridge University Press: Cambridge, 1985).

*LINDLEY, MARK, and BOXALL, MARIA, *Early Keyboard Fingerings: An Anthology* (Schott: London, 1980). Contains 14 examples of music by Bach, Handel, Couperin, Dandrieu and others, with 'extensive original indications of the fingerings'.

MACCLINTOCK, CAROL, ed. and trans., *Readings in the History of Music in Performance* (Indiana University Press: Bloomington, 1979). Anthology of contemporary writings on musical performance from the late Middle Ages to Berlioz.

MCKINNON, JAMES W., 'The 10th-century Organ at Winchester', *Organ Year Book* 5 (1974), p. 4.

MAHRENHOLZ, CHRISTHARD, *Die Orgelregister* (Bärenreiter: Kassel, 1930). A classic on the history and construction of organ-stops; German text.

MATHER, BETTY BANG, *Interpretation of French Music from 1675–1775, for Woodwind and Other Performers* (McGinnis & Marx, New York, 1973). A practical approach containing many musical examples. Additional comments on German and Italian music. Available through music shops rather than booksellers.

*MESSIAEN, OLIVIER, *Technique de mon Langage Musical* (Leduc: Paris, 1944); Eng. trans.

John Satterfield as *The Technique of My Musical Language* (1957). Text and musical examples in two volumes. (See also GRIFFITHS, PAUL).

MOZART, LEOPOLD, *Versuch einer gründlichen Violinschule* (Augsburg, 1756); trans. E. Knocker as *A Treatise on the Fundamental Principles of Violin Playing* (Oxford University Press: London, 1948).

NEUMANN, FREDERICK, *Ornamentation in Baroque and Post-Baroque Music, with Special Emphasis on J. S. Bach* (Princeton University Press: Princeton, 1978). Questions the rigid acceptance of many prevailing theories . . . more for the advanced student, and indispensable for the scholar.

—— 'Essays in Performance Practice' (UMI Research Press: Ann Arbor, 1983). Representing an anti-establishment manifesto challenging some of the best-known, most widely accepted and most influential theories on performance practice in seventeenth- and eighteenth-century music.

PADGHAM, CHARLES A., *The Well-tempered Organ* (Positif Press: Oxford, 1986). An investigation of tuning temperaments.

PARKINS, ROBERT, 'Cabezón to Cabanilles: Ornamentation in Spanish Keyboard Music', *Organ Year Book* 11 (1980), p. 5.

PEETERS, FLOR, and VENTE, M. A., *De orgelkunst in de Nederlanden* (Antwerp, 1971); Eng. trans. Peter Williams, *The Organ and its Music in the Netherlands 1500–1800* (Edinburgh, 1971). A large book in every sense, with fantastic photographs—a MUST for the better-off student's coffee-table; comes with two records.

PONT, GRAHAM, 'Handel's Overtures for Harpsichord or Organ: An Unrecognized Genre', *Early Music* 11 (1983), No. 3, p. 309.

ROUTH, FRANCIS, *Early English Organ Music from the Middle Ages to 1837* (Barrie & Jenkins: London, 1973).

ROWNTREE, J. P., and BRENNAN, J. F., *The Classical Organ in Britain*, 3 vols. (Positif Press: Oxford, 1975, 1979, 1990). Covers the years 1955–89. Organ specifications, with line drawings, photographs, and informative introductions. All mechanical-action organs.

SACHS, BARBARA, and IFE, BARRY, ed. and trans., *Anthology of Early Keyboard Methods* (*Diruta, Santa Maria, Ammerbach, Banchieri, Buchner, H. de Cabezón, Venegas*) (Gamut Publications: Cambridge, 1981).

*SCHMIEDER, WOLFGANG, *Thematisch-systematisches Verzeichnis der musikalischen Werke von Johann Sebastian Bach: Bach-Werke-Verzeichnis* [BWV] (Leipzig, 1950; Breitkopf & Härtel: Wiesbaden, 1961). The accepted thematic index of J. S. Bach's works.

SCHWEITZER, ALBERT, *J. S. Bach* (A. & C. Black: London, 1923). First published in French 1905. The classic beginning of the re-evaluation of Bach in the twentieth century.

SESSIONS, ROGER, *The Musical Experience of Composer, Performer, Listener* (Princeton University Press: Princeton, 1950).

SNYDER, KERALA J., *Dieterich Buxtehude: Organist in Lübeck* (Schirmer: New York, 1988). A scholarly, comprehensive, and very readable English-language study of this composer, performer, and entrepreneur; and an informative guide to performance practice.

SODERLUND, SANDRA, *Organ Technique: An Historical Approach* (Hinshaw, Chapel Hill, 1980; 2nd edn. 1986). A well-prepared modern tutor responding to the current American vogue for doctrinaire fingering not always related to the wider issues involved in sensitive interpretation. Probably better for the already well-read thoughtful student than for the beginner.

*SUMNER, WILLIAM L., *The Organ: Its Evolution, Principles of Construction and Use* (MacDonald: London, 1952).

SUTTON, Sir JOHN, *A Short Account of Organs Built in England from the Reign of Charles II to the Present Time* (Positif Press: Oxford, 1979). Fascimile of 1847 edn.

TAGLIAVINI, LUIGI FERDINANDO, 'The art of "not leaving the instrument empty": Comments on Early Italian Harpsichord Playing', *Early Music* 11 (1983), No. 3, p. 299.

TEMPERLEY, NICHOLAS, 'Organs in English Parish Churches 1660–1830', *Organ Year Book* 10 (1979), p. 83.

THISTLETHWAITE, NICHOLAS, '"E pur si muove": English Organ Building 1820–1851', *Organ Year Book* 7 (1976), p. 101.

—— *The Making of the Victorian Organ* (Cambridge University Press: Cambridge, 1990). A study of change in English organ-building, 1800–70, including material on repertoire, performance practice, and liturgical use. Most readable.

THOMSON, ANDREW, *The Life and Times of Charles-Marie Widor*, 1844–1937 (Oxford University Press: Oxford, 1987).

TÜRK, DANIEL GOTTLOB, *Klavierschule* (Leipzig and Halle, 1789), trans. and ed. R. H. Haggh as *School of Clavier Playing, or Instructions in Playing the Clavier for Teachers and Students* (Nebraska University Press: Lincoln and London, 1982). Together with C. P. E. Bach's *Essay* a central source for late eighteenth-century musical practice.

WERCKMEISTER, ANDREAS, *Erweiterte und verbesserte Orgel-Probe* (Frankfurt, 1698); Eng. trans. Gerhard Krapf (Sunbury, Raleigh, 1976). Werckmeister on testing and examining new organs.

*WILLIAMS, PETER, *The European Organ 1450–1850* (Batsford: London, 1966). Becoming a classic history. Good for period registration.

—— *Bach Organ Music* (BBC Music Guides: London, 1972). A short survey for the interested listener.

—— *The Organ Music of J. S. Bach* (Cambridge University Press: Cambridge, 1980, 1984). Vol. 1: BWV 525–598, 802–805, etc.; Vol. 2: BWV 599–771, etc. (the chorale-based works); *Vol. 3: a background.

—— *A New History of the Organ: From the Greeks to the Present Day* (Faber and Faber: London, 1980). '. . . a belated salute to the third edition of Hopkins and Rimbault [see above] and an attempt in its own right to bring the history of organs up to date, or at least to trace that history as I understand it' (author).

WILSON, J., *Roger North on Music: Being a Selection from his Essays written during the Years c.1695–1728* (Novello: London, 1959). Background to the period by a contemporary writer.

Organ Tutors

DAVIS, ROGER E., *The Organists' Manual* (W. W. Norton: New York and London, 1985). Intended for beginning organ students who have good piano background, this thoughtful and absorbing tutor contains instruction (on basic interpretation as well as technique), technical studies, and sixty-five short compositions (on two and three staves) ranging from Albrechtsberger to Zipoli.

GLEASON, HAROLD, *Method of Organ Playing* (6th edn., Prentice-Hall: Englewood Cliffs, 1979). A wide-ranging tutor containing basic interpretational material as well as technical training.

TREVOR, C. H., *The Oxford Organ Method* (Oxford University Press: London, 1971). Playing technique, from the beginning; lots of exercises and sensible, sympathetic comments.

Index of Works Cited

Page references in *italics* indicate that no musical example is given.

			Page references
J. S. Bach	Sonata I	BWV 525	102, 105, 110
	Sonata II	526	*39*, *78*
	Sonata III	527	100
	Sonata IV	528	*78*, 100
	Sonata V	529	64, 86, *97*, 98, 99, 103, 106
	Sonata VI	530	*50*, 86, 100, 113
	Toccata and Fugue in D minor	538	*66*
	Prelude and Fugue in G	541	105
	Fantasia and Fugue in G minor	542	66, 85, 87–8
	Prelude and Fugue in B minor	544	99
	Prelude and Fugue in G	550	*39*
	Prelude and Fugue in A minor	551	*93*
	Prelude and Fugue in E flat	552	104, *105*
	Toccata, Adagio and Fugue	564	63, 80–1
	Toccata and Fugue in E	566	*93*
	Canzona	588	*84*
	Nun komm' der Heiden Heiland	599	*96*
	Puer natus in Bethlehem	603	101
	Gelobet seist du, Jesu Christ	604	92, 102
	Der Tag, der ist so freuden-reich	605	*117*
	Vom Himmel hoch	606	96, 97
	In dulci jubilo	608	64–5
	Das alte Jahr	614	*145*
	O Lamm Gottes	618	101
	O Mensch bewein'	622	93, 101, *118*
	Erstanden ist der heil'ge Christ	628	99
	Durch Adams Fall	637	92
	Ich ruf' zu dir	639	*145*
	Meine Seele erheb't den Herren	648	112

	Kommst du nun, Jesu	650	*117*
	Schmücke dich	654	38
	Nun danket alle Gott	657	*117*
	Nun komm' der Heiden Heiland	659	81, *118*
	Nun komm' der Heiden Heiland	661	97–8
	Allein Gott in der Höh' sei Ehr'	662	113, *118*
	Allein Gott in der Höh' sei Ehr'	663	*117*
	Kyrie, Gott Vater in Ewigkeit	669	*117*
	Christe, aller Welt Trost	670	101
	Jesus Christus unser Heiland	688	*117*
	Ein' feste Burg	720	*142*
	Fugue on the Magnificat	733	97
	Canonic Variations: Vom Himmel hoch	769	*76*
	Prelude and Fugue in C minor	847	95
John Bull	Hexachord Fantasia No. 17 in *Musica Britannica* 14		*74*
D. Buxtehude	Prelude, Fugue and Ciacona	BuxWV 137	66
	Prelude and Fugue in F♯ minor	146	*24*, 85, 145
	Durch Adams Fall	183	92
	Es ist das Heil	186	63
	Gelobet seist du, Jesu Christ	189	91
	Gott der Vater	190	63–4
	Komm, heiliger Geist	199	65
F. Couperin	Messe pour les Paroisses:		
	Fugue sur les jeux d'anches		88
	Récit de Chromhorne		*120*
	Duo sur les Tierces		121
	Dialogue sur les Trompettes, etc.		122
	Benedictus—Chromhorne en taille		121
C. Franck	Fantaisie in A		133–4
J. J. Froberger	Toccata II		84
Vincent Lübeck	Prelude and Fugue in E		*93*
G. F. Handel	Organ Concerto in B flat (Op. 4, No. 6)		104

General Index

Accents, 'displaced' 81
  dynamic 142
  stress 96, 100
Acoustic, effect on line 11
Agogic accentuation 54, 65–6, 73
Alain, Jehan 134
Allegro, manner of 106
Ammerbach, E. N. 76
Antegnati, Graziado 147
Appel 155
Architecture, organ 20
Articulation 11, 16, 57 ff, 60
  caution in 106
Auden, W. H. 15
Avison, Charles 66

Bach, C. P. E. 5, 56, 73–4, 79, 88–9, 102, 105, 106, 107
Bach, J. S. 2, 3, 35, 47–8, 56, 58, 63, 72, 76, 84, 90 ff, 131, 132, 133, 149, 151
Bach, W. F. 76, 108
Bench, organ 12, 40
Blockwerk 15, 21
Bourgeois, Loys 63
Boyvin, Jacques 125
Brahms 134
Brescia, St Giuseppe 147
Britten 6
Bruhns 83, 94, 133
Buchner 74
Bull, John 74, 76
Buxtehude 1, 24, 63, 64, 65, 72, 83–4, 91–2, 94, 145, 147
Byfield, John 153
Byrd, William 75

Caccini 82
Cadence points 98
Cavaillé-Coll 40, 131, 137, 154
Chaumont, Lambert 126
Circular breathing 7

Clothing for performers 49–51
Copland 6
Corelli 2
Cornet, description 33
Corrette, Gaspard 126
Couler 124
Couperin, François 1–3, 72, 75, 77, 119, 128, 131, 153
Cunningham, G. D. 130

Dart, Thurston 11, 108
Détaché 11, 57–8, 79
Dialogue 24, 79–89
Diruta 45–6, 66, 75
Dolmetsch, Arnold 54, 67, 83, 130
Dom Bédos 24, 139 ff
Dots 100–1
Douglass 119
Dupré 134

Elst, J. van der 11
Emery, Walter 96, 109
Explication 108–9
Expression 7, 53 ff

Fantasy style (see *Stilus fantasticus*)
Fashion, dangers of 70
Feet, playing position 47–9
  shoes 50
Figura corta 87, 95 ff
Figura suspirans 96 ff
Fingering 71, 74–8
Fisk 145
Forkel 46–7, 57
Franck 3, 94, 131, 133–4, 154
Frescobaldi 2, 62, 83, 133
Froberger 83–4

Galsworthy, John 60
Gerber, Ernst 47
Glockenspiel 150, 151

Grand siècle 72, 119ff, 131
Grands jeux 125–6, 137
Grund 125

Handel 62
Hands, playing position 44–5
Hanslick, Eduard 5
Harmonic partials 29, 34
Harris, Renatus 142
Haydn, Josef 132
Hemiola 104
Hindemith 135
Hope-Jones 131

Improvisation 135
Industrial Revolution 2
Inequality (*inégalité*) 62–3, 71, 73, 78, 122–5
Interpretation 72

Jeu 125
Johnson, Samuel 5
Jordan, Abraham 142

Keller, Hermann 3
Key action 10, 13, 15–21
Kirnberger 145

Le Begue 126
Legato 11, 49, 55, 58–9, 79
Leonardo da Vinci 42–3
Line
    coinciding notes 88–9
    musical 73, 93
Liszt 134
London
    Temple Church 142, 152
Loudness, public expectation 3, 12
Lourer 122
Lübeck, Marienkirche 139
Lübeck, Vincent 93, 94

Matthay, Tobias 68
Mattheson, Johann 84
Mendelssohn 2, 35, 78, 132–3
Mersenne 58
Merulo 83
Messiaen 134

Mixtures 32, 34
Mizler 76
Monteverdi 82
Mozart, L. 37–8
Mozart, W. A. 132
Mühlhausen, St. Blasius 114, 149
Mutations 33

Nivers 1, 63, 77, 126
Nodes and antinodes 24
Notes inégales 122

Organo pleno 115, 137
Orgelbüchlein (Bach) 93–4, 96
Ornaments 107–14, 128–9
    appoggiatura (*accent, port de voix*) 109, 111–12, 129
    cadence (turn) 109, 114, 129
    closing notes 111
    mordent (*pincé*) 109, 113–14, 129
    nachschlag 108, 112 (cf. 129)
    pralltriller 110 (cf. 129)
    schneller 110
    shakes 108–11, 128
    slide 113 (cf. 129)

Pachelbel 94
Pallets 14, 16ff
Paris
    St Gervais 153
    Ste Clotilde 154
Pedals 18, 48–9
Performance, organ aids to 12, 35–7
    definitive? 69
    (*and see* Projection)
Phrasing 78
Pine, Courtney 68
Pipes 24–35
    axis of, relative to listener 18
    speech 52
Piquer (*pointer*) 124
Pitch, related to harmonics 34
Plein jeu 32, 125, 137
Pointing 55
Ponitz 150
Posture 40–1, 47–8
Praetorius 66, 71, 83

Projection, musical 53 ff
Pulse 61, 71, 96, 102–5
   placing 79–80
Purcell 62

Quantz 58, 102, 106, 111

Raison, André 2, 76, 125, 126, 127
Rameau 96
Recording 137
Reger 131, 134
Registers (*see* Stops)
Reubke 134
Rhythm 59, 60, 62, 106
Riemann, Hugo 65
Rollerboard 18, 21
Rubato 54, 67

Saint-Lambert 58
Salisbury Cathedral 142
Santa Maria, Tomas de 62, 75
Schrider, Christopher 152
Schulze 148
Schumann 134
Schütz, Heinrich 83
Servo-mechanisms 12
Sesquialtera
   proportion 104
   stop 33, 116–17, 150
Seville Cathedral 142
Shakespeare 132
Shaw, Bernard 132
Shelley 37
Silbermann, Gottfried 16, 22, 133, 137, 150
Silence 55 ff, 73, 96
Singing 6–7
Slurs 78, 100
Smith, Bernard 152
Sound quality 29–35
Speech and music 5
Staccato 59, 100
Stanley, John 152

Stilus canonicus 84
Stilus fantasticus 54, 82 ff
Stops, definition 14–15
Stravinsky 9, 68
Sumner, W. L. 131, 143
Suspensions 99
Sweelinck 1, 2, 76, 83
Swell box 36
   musical use of 142

Taste (*bon goût*) 71
Temperament 144–6
Tempo 105–6
Tempo rubato 54, 67
Tension, muscular 41
   musical 99
Terraced dynamics 24
Theatre organ 3
Thierry, Alexandre 153
Tierce en taille 117, 125–6
Tirasses 125, 145–6
Touch 16, 55–60, 73, 78
Tournemire, Charles 134
Tremulant 3, 9, 37–9, 115, 150
Tuning 24–9
Türk 67, 76

Vallotti 145
Vitruvius 42
Vivaldi 2

Walther, J. G. 95
Weckmann, Matthias 83
Weimar Castle 149
Werckmeister 145
Werkprinzip 22, 142, 148
Williams, Peter 5, 93, 96, 101, 147
Winchester organ 15
Wind 9, 14, 39

Zelenka 95